Blurtseau Lundif

Corsaire Extraordinaire

by Alan Davison

© 2014 Alan Davison - all rights reserved
the text and images that make up this book can be found at:
http://blurtso.com & http://blog.blurtso.com

Shield Publishers
ISBN-13: 978-0966144161
ISBN-10: 0966144163

Hmmm, thought Blurtso, what shall I write? Maybe a story? Maybe a tale? Maybe an epic tale, one of adventure and intrigue? Yes, an epic tale with a tragic hero... a brave and chivalrous donkey, a Renaissance donkey who sails the seas in search of fortune and fame... Hmmm, I'd better find a good opening line... yes... an opening line that makes it impossible not to read on... an irresistible line... yes, an irresistible line... Hmmm, thought Blurtso, thinking long and hard what to write... I've got it!...

"Blurtseau Lundif, the Renaissance donkey, thought long and hard what to write... but what words to address the King? What words indeed, from the pen of a renegade donkey exiled from happiness and home. Exiled, from the sight and embrace of the one who holds his heart, the purest of pure, the sweetest of sweet, the tender and ravishing Blurtsoiselle..."

"Qu'est-ce qu'on doit faire?!" shouted the cook, breaking into the galley. "The storm is coming!!"

"What shall we do?!" snapped Blurtseau, rising from the écrivan. "We shall do as always! We shall turn and face the storm!" No sooner had Blurtseau capped the inkwell and stored his pen than he heard the first wave crash on the foredeck.

"Mon Capitaine!" cried the First Mate. "Nous avons besoin de vous!"

The chaos and confusion ceased the moment the crew spied the tip of Blurtseau's nose, and by the time his ears and eyes came on deck the sailors were in line and standing at attention. Blurtseau paused for a moment in the hurricane gale, staring into the eyes of his terrified crew, then he walked slowly and steadily to the prow where he turned and cried with a voice louder than the storm, "To your posts and ride out the wind!"

"Ma chère Blurtsoiselle," wrote Blurtseau, "the storm has passed and again I am spared death and condemned to this living grave. I trust you are well. I trust the geraniums are in bloom and winter is not upon you. At sea we are bound to a seasonless season. The waves rise and fall, and the stars set our sails to a horizonless horizon. How distant this dismal barge from our afternoons at Roquebrune, eating pumpkin pie on the terrace, gazing down at the blue of the Côte d'Azur! I remember you said to me, 'Blurtseau, Je t'aime viene ce qu'y vienne,' and I too said I would never stop loving you. Ma belle Soiselle! There are no pies this year in last year's cupboard! I remain captive in the expanse of the sea, while you wander freely in the prison of your palace."

"Mon Capitaine," said the First Mate, "do not fall prey to melancholie. Exiled as we are, we may still sail in the service of our King. We may still fly the flag of France in our coeur though its colors do not dance at our mast. Courage et âme, mon Capitaine! Courage et âme! And please, mon Capitaine, do not drink so much!"

"Mon cher Pableau," said Blurtseau, "faithful First Mate of this vagrant voyage, I entreat thee, do not let the crew know of my sad and sorry state, but bar the door and say I have slipped into a deep and dreamless sleep."

"My dear Soiselle," wrote Blurtseau, "the sea is surly and the day has expired, unremarked and replaced forever. The crew grow restless in their rocking cradle, and I retreat, hoping to find you in the ink on this page. Ma chère Soiselle, I am a root entangled, a dark stone in the flickering light. Not a month, two months pass before I am reborn in your arms, but a sleepless lifetime, a slow marching of shadows. And after the words—light, wind, fire—there are only lines, paper and ink, and the repetition of repetition. I can fill the page, synchronize the sounds, and between margins try to live, but it is impossible to paint your smile, or raise a rose, with emptiness. Ma chère Soiselle! The spark grows wild in the wind! The eyes flash from the fire! Then the flower returns to the root."

"My dear Blurtseau," wrote Blurtsoiselle, "Captain of captains, slave to the sea, accept this plaintive plea from the heart that holds your heart more dear than her own. Three moons, swollen and swallowed, have marked the sky since last these eyes were warmed with words from thee. Terse and unbending in the ruffian wind... prow, mast, and rudder to his unsteady crew... only I, of all donkeys, know the willows that weep in your heart. My days unfold uncounted in the courtyard that has become my cloister. Arising at dawn, and following the sun's course like a somnambulistic sprout, I wander from corner to corner, until my shrunken world slouches to shadow, and I mourn 'til morn tugs anew at my tether. Sleepless, when the moon is full, I sit at my window, comforted that on the arms of the sea my sovereign espies the same orb in the same sky, and borrows, as the moon borrows light from the sun, strength from the star in his life that is me. My dearest of dear, mon cher Blurtseau, the King's cousin importunes daily, promising my release from this courtly captivity, if only I will admit his advances. But fear not, mon cher, that the sad Soiselle who scribbles this assurance is any other than the one who showered you with kisses the day you departed, that dismal day, when the sun fled the sky to take refuge in my heart, granting me the courage and strength to stave off the dark tolling of these dungeon days."

Unable to bear his separation from the lovely Blurtsoiselle, the Corsaire Extraordinaire, promising to meet his First Mate later in Paris, left his ship and set about to enter France through Spain. In order to confound the spies sent to prevent his return, he donned the disguise of:

"BlurtZo de la Brava Espada"

Quickly, he disappeared in the crowd…

Sleeping by day and traveling by night,
BlurtZo made his way through Castilla La Mancha…

And with the aid of Spaniards not loyal to their tyrannical King,
he found local employment
as he continued his flight to the north…

At the border, BlurtZo hired a guide
to lead him through the mountains…

And after crossing the Pyrenees, he followed a heavenly aroma
to an inn where he was attended by a jolie jeune fille.

My Lord, you look unwell. Perhaps a nap to restore your health?

And while he slept, Blurtseau Lundif was swept into the night…

Destined to awake a prisoner in the dungeon at Versailles. Convicted and condemned to death by guillotine, BlurtZo was granted one last request. Cleverly, he ordered a pumpkin pie from the newest and most popular bakery in Paris, the "Boulangerie Pableau."

Knowing the pie had been drugged, BlurtZo insisted the guard take a slice for himself, and when the guard was lying unconscious on the floor, BlurtZo seized the moment...

And finished the half-eaten pie.

Fortunately, when BlurtZo awoke the jailer was still sleeping, and our hero slipped out of his cell and into the magnificent gardens of Versailles.

"Mon Dieu!" said the gardener. "That donkey has escaped from the Queen's hamlet and is eating the royal shrubbery! I must return him at once!"

"Bonjour mon âne," said the Queen, "are you hungry?"
"My Queen!" cried the King's page, bursting into the garden. "The peasants are angry because they have no bread!"

"Don't bother me!" snapped the Queen. "If they have no bread, let them eat pumpkin pie!"

And so it was that Blurtseau, stuffing himself daily, remained at the Queen's hamlet until one afternoon…

"My Queen!" cried the King's page, "the King's cousin is returning to town and asks if you would join him?"

Moving with an agility uncommon to any creature who had just consumed a dozen pumpkin pies, Blurtseau leapt from a shrubbery, scaled the rear of the coach, and locked onto the luggage rack as the carriage sped off to Paris. "Blurtsoiselle," he thought, "my heart has wings, and I am as light as a feather!"

Blurtseau's heart was as light as a feather, but his stomach was as heavy as a stone, and he soon fell asleep atop the coach. Then, moments before reaching the cousin's logement, he was thrown from the carriage.

When he awoke, he continued on hoof into the city… then he saw her. The purest of pure, the sweetest of sweet, the tender and ravishing Blurtsoiselle! For a moment their eyes met... it was the moment he had dreamed of, the light that had sustained him, the breath that had filled his hours of exile, travel, and torment, it was... too much for his heart to bear, and he fell down hooves up and senseless in the gutter. Had he not been paralyzed and un-

conscious, he might have mistaken her glance for the most tender gaze that ever donkey gazed in the history of donkeys, as Blurtsoiselle looked down on our fallen hero whose mouth was slowly filling with the water that ran in the street. But the fearless corsaire saw not this gaze, nor did he see Blurtsoiselle fourteen hours later when he awoke, half-drowned and still shivering, in the Boulangerie of his faithful first mate, Pableau la Chanson.

"Je suis désolé," said Blurtseau. "I've been in Paris three weeks and have not managed to get a word to the lovely Blurtsoiselle!"

"Peut-être," said Pableau, "I have an idea! Write a note on this wrapper, and I will deliver your words with a pastry to her lodging. I will say the pastry was ordered by Blurtsoiselle. The King's cousin will surely accept the envoi!"

"Brilliant," said Blurtseau. "We'll send her petits choux chantilly! Petits choux pour mon petit chou!"

"Mon Dieu," said Pableau, "What a poet you are!"

A drop of rain that falls
is more fortunate than I.

Your blanket and tether,
and all the things you touch,
are far more fortunate than I.

The grass beneath your hoof
is more fortunate than I.

What you hear, what hears you,
is much more fortunate than I.

The bird at your window,
the walls of your room,
the pillow that catches
your whispering bray.

Everything that sees you,
the sun breaking through,
the dogs and the cats,
and the sleepy coachman
waiting at your door,
are far more fortunate than I.

Your mirror is infinitely fortunate.

A drunk on the stoop
squints to see you pass,
and is far more fortunate than I.

Mon cher petit chou,

The restless orb rises, carving the city in shadows and spreading its aurum on the Seine. We are apart. The many-colored sparks scatter and reveal the scarred face of the stream, and the weaving water clock marks what is lost... a memory walking along the quai, your shadow and mine, stretching to the beginning behind us, our gaze set on the future ahead... a memory we will never have. Alone, I turn and walk back, a single shadow, searching for a time and place, when we were together...

> As the weeks passed, Blurtseau continued to write,
> even when he received no reply...

Ma chère Soiselle,

Again I pause to compose your daily note. And again I wait, but receive no reply. The days have become weeks, and the weeks have become months, and with each passing minute I pass a timeless eternity. You will not write. You will not be seen at your window. And the faithful messenger who delivers my notes, meets only the chambermaid at your door. I am adrift on a sea of doubt, and there is no shore in sight.

Respectfully,
your supplicant and servant,
Blurtseau L'un d'If

and then one day, the reply arrived…

My dear Blurtseau,

With heavy hoof I inscribe the sounds you have long feared to hear. I am gone. I have fled with the cousin of the King. I am his, and he is mine. Proximity has conquered distance. Despite the pain this will cause, I hope we can still remain friends.

adieu,
Blurtsoiselle

Blurtseau Lundif could not believe what his eyes had read. It was as if he was deciphering a language he did not understand and his guess at its meaning was surely mistaken. He read the words again. And again. Finally, he realized the letter was not written in a foreign tongue, and he did comprehend its meaning, and Blurtsoiselle was indeed saying what her words were saying, and she had given her heart to another, and her affections, and her soul which had been the North Star guiding Blurtseau through his endless nights. And he was annihilated. "I must find Pableau!" he said out loud. "For if I do not find a pair of loving eyes to assure me I am alive, I will simply cease to exist." And in his greatest moment of misfortune, fortune was near, and when he cried out, "I must find Pableau!"

Pableau—who had just returned from his morning errands—heard his friend's cry and rushed to his side, saying, "Here I am my friend, here is your dear and trusted friend Pableau." And those thirteen words were, for an annihilated soul on the edge of extinction, a silver thread which Blurtseau grasped with every fiber of his being, knowing that if he held on, and never let go, that the thread would slowly restore him to the world of the living. "My friend," said Blurtseau, "I who have been reduced to ashes and rubble, and scarcely have a breath to offer, owe you the world." And the two donkeys embraced, as if clutching to life itself, amidst the boulangerie smells of flour, yeast, and baking bread.

Blurtsoiselle,

I have received your letter and overcome its contents. Logically, I can concede the ravages of distance and time, and the dispassionate mind can imagine how you have arrived at your state and place. But sadly, what the mind might imagine, the heart struggles to comprehend. Perhaps the image I forged of you was not a being meant for the reality perceived by you or by me. We have reached the fork, and we have parted. You shall remain in your world, and I shall remain in mine. You ask that we remain friends. Am I to pretend I do not feel what I feel? I'm sorry, but an honest heart knows only its honest ways.

Farewell,
Blurtseau L'un d'If

And Blurtseau considered the past. Must it now be erased? Must he sponge out the vanquished hopes and dreams and memories of moments in the eye of the storm when he and Blurtsoiselle had sat together, saying little, doing less, gazing out on a common tomorrow? Must the canvas be painted over in dusky black and grey? And to go on? To live? What reason to wake at dawn, and attempt to sleep at night? A single thought buoyed him; his love for Pableau. Blurtseau knew that his friend was concerned for his welfare, and that Blurtseau's pain had become his pain as well. He knew if he truly loved his friend, he would have to do better. And with that one thought, Blurtseau recognized his obligation on the other end of the thread, the thread with which Pableau had saved him, and that was to console his friend by consoling himself. And so it was that our Corsaire Extraordinaire, Blurtseau Lundif and BlurtZo de la Brava Espada, reached into his own sad heart and pulled himself up, firmly, from the depth of despair. Then, with teeth clenched and steady on his hooves, he rose from his chair, embraced his friend, and walked into the day.

"Hurry my Lord!" shouted Pableau. "The gendarmes are coming! We must flee!"

"Ahhh," said Blurtseau, rising slowly from the écrivan, "the King's henchmen have found me. Flee? No, mon cher, not before my sword is drunk with traitors' blood." And so saying, Blurtseau seized his mask and cape and rushed to meet his fate.

What happened next is recorded reluctantly in the annals of history, for it can be scarcely believed. Moving with the speed of a wildcat, Blurtseau burst into the salon and sprang upon his enemies. He was here, he was there, he was here, there, here, there, there, here, here, there, fighting with the fury of ten Blurtseaus, plus two…

In less than fourteen minutes the soldiers were routed. Blurtseau searched the chamber for a sign of the King's cousin, but, finding none, abandoned the salon, darted into the street, and boarded the carriage pulled by his ever-faithful friend.

Blurtseau and Pableau sped from Paris to Hendaye, Hendaye to Lisbon, and Lisbon to Sagres, where they took refuge in the fortress of Blurtseau's historic idol, Henry the Navigator. Here, at the end of the earth, Blurtseau could begin to console his convalescing heart….

"Yes," thought Blurtseau, "a soul could yearn here."

In Sagres our heroes quickly secured lodgings and got the lay of the land at a local bar. Fearing that spies were still on their trail, they purchased a fishing vessel to take up the local trade, and in no time they were indistinguishable from the residents of Sagres…

"Hey!" said Blurtseau. "Is that a pumpkin patch?!"

As the days passed Blurtseau filled the hours with fishing, surfing and drinking, until one day he found himself staring at the sea… he remembered his first job as an apprentice sailor in Marseilles, ferrying goods to the Château d'If. Once a week for seven years he journeyed there, loaded with fruit, bread, and meat. He knew that the prisoners tasted only the leftovers discarded by the guards—rotten fruit, moldy bread, meat too rancid to be swallowed—but Blurtseau was young, and he thought only of his fortune at having secured the job. He readily accepted his nickname "L'un d'If," given him by the longshoremen when they greeted him upon returning from the Château, as a badge of honor, and promised to wear it the length of his days.

His happiest times were after he had unloaded his cargo, and his unburdened skiff could ride the winds back to Marseilles. The afternoon light made the city shine, like a crown atop the harbor, and he was struck with the irony that only the guards, and prisoners with windowed cells, could look upon the beautiful scene.

He also remembered his first bonafide tour, aboard the Ésperance, learning the ropes and getting his sea hooves beneath him. He thought of all who had helped him along the way, lending an ear, or shoulder, or laugh, and of those who had not. By the time he made First Mate he was sailing regularly to Tunis and Algiers, and it was then he met Pableau, the starry-eyed ensign whose heart spoke to him. A year later, when Blurtseau received his first command, he knew that the only sailor he could trust with his life was Pableau, and he hired him on as First Mate for six years in the Navy of the King. Then Blurtseau fell in love.

There was a ball thrown by the King for the captains and admirals of his fleet, and all the world changed when Blurtseau's eyes met the eyes of Blurtsoiselle. Unfortunately, the King's cousin set his eyes on the same prize, and from that moment forward the King received damning reports of Blurtseau's conduct aboard his caravel. There were accusations of volunteerism, embezzlement, and misuse of goods, and most damning of all, faithlessness and fraternizing with the enemies of France. Soon after, Blurtseau lost his commission, and would have lost his ship, had he not got wind of the news and sequestered the vessel. Branded as renegade and outlaw, he continued to sail, flagless, with his faithful crew and trusty Mate, in the service of his Lord.

Blurtseau thought of all these things as he watched the dying light flicker on the sea. He knew that the book of his youth was closed, its pages would be consulted no more, and it was time to write a new tale—hoist a new sail—and find a new beacon to illuminate his possibility-filled pages…

"I'm finished untangling this net," said Blurtseau.
"How about you? Tu es prêt?"

"Pas encore…"

Let's see, thought Blurtso. My Renaissance donkey has displayed his prowess in poetry and battle, and has shown his loyalty, even in exile, to his beloved France. Now he must hold forth on science, philosophy, and matters of state:

"Do you believe we will return to France?" said Pableau.

"La France?" said Blurtseau. "Ahhh, ma mère que me manque comme une jambe que je l'ai perdue.... la France... A time of change is in the offing… the King, whose favor I've lost, sits an uneasy throne. Revolution is ahoof. The people starve and the Queen fattens pets with her pies. I know, for I am as guilty as she. I have used infatuation as an excuse to ignore. But we live in an age of Reason, and the people will be heard."

"Who will govern," said Pableau, "when the King is gone?"

"Who?" said Blurtseau. "A warrior, a poet, a prophet, a seer with a pirate's principles and a maiden's heart."

"A pirate's principles?" said Pableau.

"Yes," said Blurtseau. "For of all seamen, only the pirate practices democracy. Only there, aboard his ship, is each one alike, and all booty divided evenly. The captain rules, as he must, with an iron hoof, but his authority rests on the vote of his mates, and his tenure may not outlast the gale."

"And a maiden's heart?" said Pableau.

"Yes," said Blurtseau. "A heart made of constancy, compassion, and the hopefulness that springs from innocence."

"Will you be the one?" asked Pableau. "Will you be the savior of France?"

"No," said Blurtseau. "I am but a child of the mother that bore me. And though I may lord over the ship I sail, the helm of France is reserved for a hoof more willful, and more determined, than my own."

"Oh," said Pableau.

"You never told me why you decided to become a sailor," said Blurtseau.

"There's not much to tell," said Pableau.

"Bof!" said Blurtseau, "everyone has a tale."

"Well," said Pableau, "my story begins in northern France… in fact… I wrote a song about it."

"A song?" said Blurtseau. "May I hear it?"

"As you wish," said Pableau. "It goes like this…

"The fog is low on the morning fields
and the village bells are ringing,
the voices of the birds I know so well
will soon be singing…

I stand in the door on the floor
that's worn out my hooves,
and dream of a place
I can live the life I choose.
I've heard tales of lands
and people across the sea,
and I know that beyond
these hills...
is a kingdom meant for me.

I've been living the life of a child seeking approval and reward,
leaving others to make my decisions and my future unexplored,
but this aching inside is a voice I can't dismiss,
if I don't want to spend my life wondering what I've missed.
The time has come for self-responsibility,
time to take my chances to the kingdom meant for me.

I know these fields and houses, every alley and every lane,
they've told me who I am and tied me to my name,
but I know that there'll be more than this to me,
if I shake off these reins and follow my curiosity.
It's hard to believe in what I cannot see,
but I must believe if I'm going to find the kingdom meant for me.

Will I manage the changing seasons, will I wither or be reborn?
Will my offerings be outcast, my resolve be outworn?
Will I have the strength to answer when my demons call?

Will solitude devour me, will someone help me if I fall?
When the night is black will I be able to see
if I'm on the road to disaster or to the kingdom meant for me?

The bells have stopped ringing and the workers are in the fields,
the fog has finally lifted and the horizon has been revealed.
I don't know if I'll be back this way again,
but there's a part of me here that will always remain.
The sun is warm and shining above the trees,
and it's high time I departed to the kingdom meant for me."

"The breeze has stopped," said Pableau, "and it's suddenly quiet. I wonder where the people are?"

"They're probably at home," said Blurtseau.

"At home?" said Pableau.

"Yes," said Blurtseau, "like us."
"Oh," said Pableau, "they must be very happy."

As thoughts of France faded in the sound of the wind and the waves, discussions of honor, justice, and national obligation were replaced by less-weighty concerns… "Blurtseau," said Pableau, "do you think I'm fat?"

"The local wine is very good," said Pableau.
"Yes," said Blurtseau, "it goes well with the country."
"I wonder," said Pableau, "if the country was developed to go

with the wine, or if it was the wine that was developed to go with the country?"

"That's a good question," said Blurtseau.

"Yes, it is," said Pableau.

"Would you like another glass of the country?" asked Blurtseau.

"Yes," said Pableau, "to go with the wine."

"The sun is not so high," said Pableau.

"No," said Blurtseau, "it isn't."

"I suppose it's later," said Pableau.

"Yes," said Blurtseau, "later."

"The breeze is soft on the ears," said Pableau.

"Very soft," said Blurtseau.

"I wonder what's happening in France," said Pableau.

"It's hard to imagine," said Blurtseau.

Coming as he did from a long line of chefs, Pableau did the cooking, and he was assiduous. Every morning he would go to market to select the ingredients for the day's repast, taking care to pick only the healthiest lettuce, the juiciest tomatoes, and the freshest bread for his bag. One day, as he was reaching for his favorite pastry, a petit chou chantilly, his eyes spied the most beautiful hoof he had ever seen.

"Goodness me!" he thought. "How extraordinary!" Then he let his glance continue to an even lovelier limb, and shoulder, and neck, and ear, and… then the vendor announced a sale on tomatoes and everything disappeared in a crowd of limbs and ears. But later that night Pableau thought of the hoof, and the jenny that went with it. He thought, "She is out there somewhere, beyond the wind at my door.  She is out there, speaking, breathing, and moving about. I will have to find her. Yes, he thought, I will have to find her."

"I saw a hoof yesterday," said Pableau, "at market."

"A hoof?" said Blurtseau.

"Yes," said Pableau. "We were reaching for the same petit chou chantilly."

"Oh," said Blurtseau, "petit chou chantilly!"

"It was the most beautiful thing I've ever seen," said Pableau.

"The chantilly?" said Blurtseau.

"No," said Pableau, "the hoof."

"Did you manage to seize it?" said Blurtseau.

"The chantilly?" said Pableau.

"No," said Blurtseau, "the hoof."

"No," said Pableau.

"That's too bad," said Blurtseau.
"I may never see another one like it," said Pableau.
"The chantilly?" said Blurtseau.
"No," said Pableau, "the hoof."

"There it goes!" cried Pableau.
"There goes what?" said Blurtseau.
"The hoof!" said Pableau. "It's on the road to Évora!"

And so, while Blurtseau stayed behind, Pableau, with only his heart to guide him, started down the road to Évora, in search of a hoof.

And on he went, through the olive and cork forests…

Until he reached Évora.

Certain that everyone in Évora must be familiar with the most beautiful hoof in the world, Pableau went in search of his Cinderella…

"Human bones? Whew! For a minute I thought they were donkey bones!"

"They're even building her a temple."

When it became apparent that Pableau was not going to find the enchanted hoof in a day, or a week, or perhaps even a month, he decided to seek employment at one of the local bakeries. In this, fortune was with him, for the first bakery he approached needed someone to work the morning shift, opening the shop and firing the ovens. As the days passed, Pableau noticed that a certain villa, or "quinta" as he learned to call it, had a standing order for a dozen petit chou chantillies to be delivered daily. Hoping against hope that the consumer of those dozen chantillies might be the self-same shopper whose hoof he had spied reaching for a chantilly in Sagres, he ventured out to the quinta.

When he arrived, he was met at the gate by the gatekeeper, who informed him he could not pass. Fortunately, Pableau had brought a special chantilly into which he had managed to insert a triple helping of whipped cream, and when the guard saw the magnificent treat, he accepted it in exchange for Pableau's entry to the grounds.

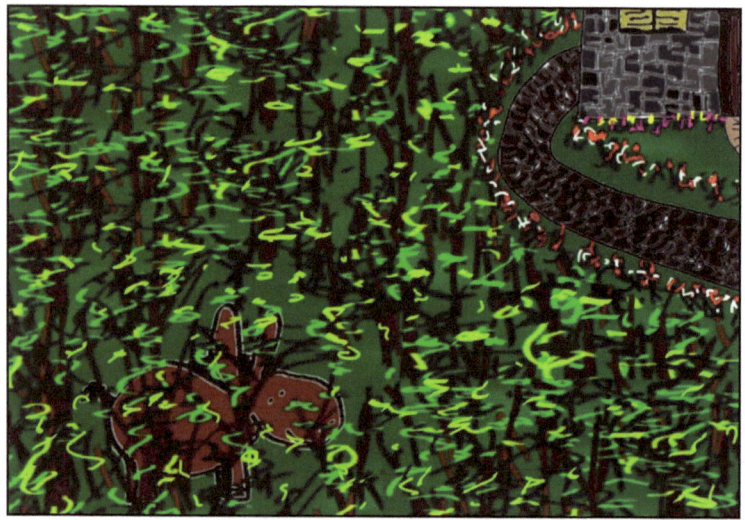

The love-sick baker spent the entire day watching the door of the house, which opened on several occasions, taking his breath away each time, but not once did he see the magical hoof. Finally, tired and discouraged, he returned to the bakery and his room at the back of the shop.

The day dawned damp and chilly, long after Pableau had risen from his water-logged straw to fire the bakery ovens. He had been toiling for hours when the first customers arrived, and by then the air in the shop was warm and dry, and even the cracks in the walls were thick with the scent of bread. Although it had been more than three months since his arrival, and though his excursion to the villa had been in vain, Pableau's resolve remained firm, for despite his repeated failures he knew that the story of the boulanger in search of the hoof was making its way around town, and that notice of his existence would eventually fall upon the ears of the one he sought.

He was consoling himself with this hopeful, patient logic as he placed a fresh tray of chantillies in the pastry window, when a carriage suddenly appeared on the street, and before he could comprehend what was happening, he saw the most beautiful donkey in the world descend from the coach…

"Are you Pableau the baker?" she asked, when she had stepped inside.

"Yes," said Pableau, "I am."

"And you have been seeking me for over three months?"

"Yes," said Pableau, "I have."

"Having seen only my hoof? And having seen it on only three occasions?"

"Yes," said Pableau.

"And you have been discovered in the garden of my quinta," she said, "by my eyes and others', skulking about the shrubberies?"

"That," said Pableau, "I cannot say, for your eyes may well have seen me, but mine, sadly, did not see you. But yes, he continued, I was indeed on the grounds, for I bribed the gatekeeper to let me pass."

"I see," said Zurrabela, "and now, may I know what you expect of me?"

"I expect nothing," said Pableau, "I only hope."

"Hope?" said Zurrabela. "And what do you hope?"

"I hope," said Pableau, "that yours is the heart I am seeking, and that mine is the heart you seek."

"But," said Zurrabela, "that hope is without reason, for you have sought only a hoof."

"Yes," said Pableau, "that is true, but I know my heart, and my heart knows reasons that reason knows not."

"But how can you be sure," said Zurrabela, "that I seek any heart at all?"

"I cannot be sure," said Pableau, "I can only hope."

"Yes," said Zurrabela, "as you have said… may I know how long you will lodge in Évora?"

"Until my dreams are answered," said Pableau, "or until they expire."

To this last statement Zurrabela did not respond, but only gazed at the flour-covered donkey who had searched for her, tirelessly, having seen only a hoof. Pableau, too, remained silent, meeting her glance with one of his own, a glance that was open, unguarded, and fortified with conviction. Then Zurrabela made a motion to speak, but stopped, collected herself, and left the shop. Pableau remained inside, watching to see if she would make herself seen at the window of her coach, but she did not; instead he saw only what he already knew, an incomparable hoof, waving to the driver, in a gesture to depart.

It took Pableau more than seven days to recover from the impact of Zurrabela's visit, and when he began to work again, his concentration was in short supply…

Over and over, he relived the encounter. And her words rang true. He did not know her. He had been chasing a hoof. Reluctantly, he had to consider whether his infatuation was more about him than it was about her. Yes, she had struck a note within him, but it was a note that had been waiting to be struck, and though it reverberated in every fiber of his being, she might feel nothing at all. But still… and despite all that… it was Zurrabela who had struck that note… Zurrabela and only Zurrabela.

One morning when Pableau opened the bakery there was a note on the door…

"Meet me at midnight at the University."

The University of Évora, a beacon of learning run by Jesuit priests for over two hundred years, was closed in 1759 when the ideas of the Enlightenment were deemed to be too dangerous for the town's faithful. As a result, the building to which Pableau had been invited, and in which Zurrabela was anxiously waiting, had been closed for thirty years. When Pableau arrived, Zurrabela revealed her location with the softest and sweetest bray that Pableau had ever heard. Walking blindly, he followed the thread of sound until he came upon its Ariadne, and the two entered the building and made their way down a long corridor to the University library…

Once they were alone with the books,
Zurrabela closed and bolted the door.

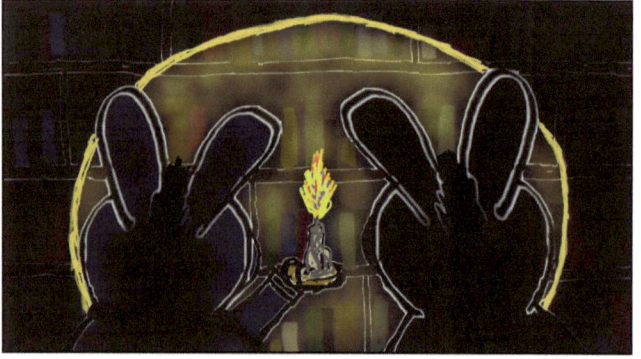

Then she lit a candle that bathed the intruders
in a circle of light…

"So that you know the risk you run," said Zurrabela, "I must tell you who I am. I am María Diana Sofía, third cousin to the Queen of Portugal, who, in case of my unlikely ascension to the throne, is being tutored by a Jesuit priest posing as a servant. My true identity has been kept secret to protect me from being sequestered for the ransom I would bring, and for that reason you must always call me Zurrabela, the nickname given me shortly after I was born.

"Before this University was closed, the crestfallen priest that is now my servant managed to slip away with a master key that opens every door of the building. I removed that key from his chain so that we could meet here tonight. If all goes well, and if you so desire, we may meet again tomorrow, and the night after that, from midnight until three strokes of the bell, at which time I must return to my quinta, replace the key on the chain, and sleep until I am awakened.

"Our meetings must become known to no one, for I am born to bear the mantel of royalty, and cannot be seen in the presence of a bloodline beneath my own. For the duration of our encounters, we will have the company of one another, as well as the company of an estimable collection of literature from the countries bordering the Mediterranean. While I do not expect you to be conversant in all the tongues in which these works are written, I myself am versed in Greek, Latin, Italian, Spanish, French, and of course Portuguese, and will gladly and patiently illuminate the magic of these pages so that, together, we might forge a bond made of wisdom and beauty. In return, I ask only to hear from you of the world beyond my quinta, of the travels you have undertaken and the adventures you have had, for I have lived a cloistered life, and my heart and mind are yearning for a draught of free and open air."

Pableau listened to all that Zurrabela had to say without interrupting, and when she was finished he said, "My esteemed Zurrabela—and I use only the name you request—you will find in me a grateful student of all that you have to teach, and an enthusiastic reporter of the life I have lived. Although the better part of glory in the adventures I have known belongs to my best friend—captain of the vessels upon which I have served—nevertheless, the tales I have to tell are replete with generous quantities of joy, excitement, and despair, and will transport you far from the captivity you have borne.

"I promise," he concluded, "that you will find me here, faithfully, each night at the stroke of twelve, and that I shall remain at your side until the third bell rings, at which time, as you have said, you must return to the cloister that awaits you."

With this, Pableau offered Zurrabela his hoof, which she accepted by offering her own, and when that lovely extremity—object of his dreams—was placed thus before him, he took it gently, looked her in the eyes and said, "Contrato feito," to which Zurrabela replied, "Contrato feito."

Hmm, thought Blurtso, looking up from the page, if Zurrabela is going to teach Greek and romance languages, and masterpieces of occidental literature, I'd better know something about those things. I wonder if Harvard offers classes in language and literature?

"Come Odysseus, said Calypso, enter my cave…
you will not be disappointed by the delights within."

"Rocinante wandered off to amuse himself with the queen's
mare, while Sancho's grey befriended the servant's mule…"

"Paolo read in a slow, steady voice...
until Francesca took the book from his hands,
and that night they read no further…"

Meanwhile, Blurtseau continued to relax
and enjoy the hospitality of Sagres…

Until one day he knew... it was time to return to sea.

Mon cher Pableau,

My heart was gladdened by your last letter and the description of your lovely Beatrice. May the horizon which now opens before you be filled with fortune and faith. I, for my part, have once again heard the call of the sea, and am anxious to respond. With no fixed course to pursue, I have decided to journey to the town of my birth. As such, the preparations are being made, and I will sail for Marseilles in three weeks time. Before departing, I would relish the opportunity to see my dear and faithful friend, and am prepared to journey to Evora to effect the reunion. Please leave word where you can be found with the town prefect, and I will inquire of him upon arriving.

Your dear friend in past, present, and future,
Blurtseau L'un d'If

    Immediately upon receiving his friend's letter, Pableau wrote to the one who owned his heart, entreating her to forgive his absence for the time it takes to journey to Sagres and back, then engaged a carriage headed for the southern coast.

"Pableau," said Blurtseau.
"Yes?" said Pableau.
"Would you do me a favor?"
"Certainly," said Pableau.
"Would you sing that song I like, the one about the cliffs?"
"Avec plaisir," said Pableau.

"I stand alone on the rocks, at the edge of the stormy sea,
watching the ships depart, sailing away from me,
they're off to seek some other land,
and once again I can't understand,
why love can never last, and the future repeats the past,
and the waves continue to crash, at the cliffs of my heart.

The sea birds hang in the air, riding the rising wind,
reminding me of the times I thought I could fly with them,
but I've lost everything that I've found,
and I'm stranded here on the ground,
'cause every flight leads to a fall, until there's nothing left at all,
except the echoes of love that call, at the cliffs of my heart.

I've learned after all of these years,
that when the light of day disappears,

you can't expect someone else to soothe all your fears,
'cause every flight leads to a fall, until there's nothing left at all,
except the echoes of love that call, at the cliffs of my heart.

I stand alone on the rocks, at the edge of the stormy sea,
watching the ships depart, sailing away from me,
they're off to seek some other land,
and once again I can't understand,
why love can never last, and the future repeats the past,
and all my hopes have been dashed, at the cliffs of my heart."

"Saudade," said Blurtseau.
"Yes," said Pableau, "saudade."

And so it was that the next day, as Pableau returned to Évora, Blurtseau headed home to the Château d'If:

"Hmm… it's not as cheery as I remember."

"Ahhhh, Marseilles... home at last!"

But Blurtseau's respite was short-lived, for no sooner had he made contact with his former crew than he got troubling news from Paris: the working class, unable to make ends meet, had stormed the Bastille, demanding a new government and threatening the life of the King. Blurtseau, having remained loyal to the King, was now despised by the revolutionaries as a loyalist, and, still burdened with the accusations that had occasioned his exile, despised by the loyalists as a traitor. His situation had become markedly more perilous, for he was suddenly pursued from all quarters.

"Once again," he said to himself, "I must flee my beloved Marseilles." And so it was that he slipped out of town—without a word to his friends whose lives he didn't want to endanger with the knowledge of his whereabouts—and started down the coast to the only place he could take refuge without being betrayed by the locals—the terraced hills of Roquebrune.

When he reached his destination—familiar site of happier days—Blurtseau slipped into an alley, then, when the coast was clear, stepped into the street. "Ahhh, Blurtsoiselle!" he sighed, remembering the time they had spent there. "How different we have become, while these stones and structures—and even the shadows—remain the same!"

"I'd better stay in the hills," thought Blurtseau, after making his way through Roquebrune. "I'll be less conspicuous there. Of course, I'll have to change my name."

"Bonjour monsieur âne," said Josette. "Comment vous appellez vous?"

"Bonjour," said Blurtseau. "Je m'appelle Jacques Lundif."

"Enchantée," said Josette. "Je suis Josette."

"Enchanté," said Jacques Lundif.

And so it was that Blurtseau Lundif—"Corsaire Extraordinaire," became Jacques Lundif—"Âne de la Montagne."

"Come," said Josette, "and help me gather flowers. Then we'll take them to town and swap them for food."

"Allons-y!"

Meanwhile, Pableau and Zurrabela left Évora and set out on their own, making their way through Spain disguised as street musicians. Zurrabela, trained in Spanish dance, and Pableau, a genius on the accordion, managed to earn enough reales to buy wine and cheese by performing a series of four-hoofed flamenco combinations.

Blurtseau continued to explore the coast...

from Monaco to Menton.

"If I had a boat, he thought, I could help Josette sell her flowers."

Josette Delacroix was a nine-year-old orphan whose mother and father had been killed in a bread-line riot in Paris. After her parents' demise she had lived in the streets, fighting with the masses for the discarded crumbs that fell from the tables of the rich. One day, while begging in front of a famous bakery, the good-hearted boulanger took pity on her and, after hearing her sad story, bought her a ticket to Marseilles with a subsequent  passage to Monaco. From there she made her way to Roquebrune and the home of her only living relative, her maternal grandfather.

Claude Depardieu, a retired naval officer, accepted his granddaughter's arrival with enthusiasm, looking upon her as a sea-weary sailor would gaze upon the beam of a distant lighthouse. The two became quick and complementary confidants; the retired captain, taciturn and morose, and the young girl, a stream of songs, smiles and chatter. Josette's spirit was reborn on the Côte d'Azur, and her life in Paris, with its soiled streets and daily sorrows, quickly became a distant memory. But her

new life was not without struggle, for Claude's pension was insufficient to cover the basic necessities, and the lords of Monaco, aware of the growing turmoil in Paris and knowing they could no longer bank on the seasonal migration of tourists from the north, raised the property taxes on their subjects in Roquebrune and Menton. Even the "common" lands, where the peasants were accustomed to gather firewood and graze their flocks, were now usurped, and the trespassers who ventured onto them did so at their own risk. Nevertheless, and despite the admonitions of her grandfather, Josette continued to visit the forbidden fields, for it was there she could gather the most colorful and fragrant flowers.

Blurtseau, still dissembling his identity as "Jacques" Lundif, was a welcome addition. He was a continual joy to the girl, who found in him a cheerful companion for her sojourns into the hills and on her trips into town, and he was a welcome conversationalist for the sailor, enlivening the evenings spent around the warmth of the fire.

"Il y avait un temps…"

With Blurtseau at her side, Josette was able to find new ways to augment the household budget. On Mondays and Thursdays she sold firewood door to door…

On Tuesdays and Fridays she did chores in a neighboring villa…

On Wednesdays she did house work…

And on weekends she sold flowers at the market in Menton.

"Who?" said Josette.
"Jean-Jacques Rousseau," said Blurtseau.

"Really?" said Josette. "You could teach me to read?"

"L'âne est un animal. Il est noble et sauvage."

Despite the decree from Monaco, Blurtseau and Josette continued to harvest wood from the forest near Roquebrune, until one day the Lords of Grimaldi, enraged that the peasants were ignoring the stricture, unleashed their hell-hounds in an attempt to clear the common lands. But the hounds soon discovered they were no match for, "La bête de la forêt."

From that time forward, on preordained days made known only to the peasants, "La bête de la forêt" would suddenly appear, swinging from tree to tree and howling like a banshee, distracting the four-legged sentries so the farmers could gather their precious fuel.

But with each passing week the news from Paris became more and more alarming. The King and Queen, having been caught attempting to flee France, were now living with their son, the Dauphin, imprisoned in the palace of the Tuilleries, while Blurtseau's arch-enemy, cousin of the King and donkeynapper of the loveliness that had stolen Blurtsteau's heart, had left Paris and abandoned Blurtsoiselle. The radical arm of the Revolution, inflamed by the rhetoric of Marat and Danton, had emptied the jails, slaughtering the men and women being held as "enemies of France," and murdering thousands of common criminals in the process. A tidal wave had been unleashed, and it was only a matter of time before the heads of the King and Queen would roll.

Monaco and the Grimaldis, intent on maintaining their independent standing, declined to join the monarchs of Spain, England, and Austria who condemned the Revolution, and opted to hold their tongue lest they should lose it if Monaco be annexed by France. Prince Honoré III hurried home to proclaim that the lands near Roquebrune would once again be open to woodcutters and farmers, and that the recently-levied taxes would be repealed. He went on to announce that the "bête de la forêt" would not be pursued for his crimes against the state, and that the hellhounds would be withdrawn from the forests.

The measures succeeded in calming the anxious populace, but all eyes and ears remained fixed on the events in Paris. Blurtseau heard the news from the capital with a mixture of sadness, anger, and concern, but when he heard that England, his country's most hated enemy, was threatening to invade under the pretext of restoring the monarchy, he rose to his hooves and declared, "Vive la France! Avec le Roi ou sans le Roi!"

And he swore an oath to all who could hear that he would fight—to his last dying bray—to defend his homeland against any invader trespassing from any foreign land.

"Is that pound cake I smell?"

"I swear I can smell pound cake."

"What did you do before you returned to Roquebrune?"
"I was a sailor," said Blurtseau.
"A sailor?" said Josette. "Like my grandfather?"
"Yes," said Blurtseau.
"How exciting!" said Josette. "Could you teach me to sail?"
"Sure," said Blurtseau, "as soon as we can afford a boat."

As the weeks passed Blurtseau became more and more comfortable in his new life, but the recent events in Paris continued to trouble his heart. The King and Queen were dead, the capital had become a slaughterhouse, and everywhere ruthlessness carried the day. The principles that had guided his life, based on the certainties of right and wrong, and love for country, were not to be found. What was right for France? Was it Robespierre? Was it another? How could the people consent to be governed by majority, when they were accustomed to obeying a king? Before, it had been easy to sail in the service of France, fighting enemies abroad, but now the fight was within, and it was hard to tell friend from foe. If only Blurtseau could see Pableau, and hear of his ongoing courtship with Zurrabela. That was a story that made sense, a story that had a future, and could be measured with clear and comforting labels. Yes, if only Blurtseau could see his dear friend Pableau.

One day, when Blurtseau was out for a walk, he smelled a familiar smell. "That smells like a petit chou Chantilly," he said, sniffing his way up the alley. "And that smells like a baguette, and that smells like a Madeleine, and that's an éclair!"

"Pableau?" "Blurtseau?" "Pableau!" "Blurtseau!"
Two happier donkeys the alleys of Roquebrune had never seen.

And there was much rejoicing.

At home there was another surprise. "Pableau?" said Josette.

"Josette?" said Pableau.

"Pableau!" said Josette.

"Josette!" said Pableau.

"What are you doing here?" said Josette.

"Well," said Pableau, "after I paid your way to see your grandfather, Zurrabela and I had to leave Paris when our bakery was raided for bread. We went to Marseilles to look for Blurtseau, and one of his crew told us he had returned to Roquebrune."

"Blurtseau?" said Josette. "Who's Blurtseau?"

"I'm Blurtseau," said Blurtseau. "My true name is Blurtseau Lundif."

"Blurtseau Lundif?" said Claude. "The 'Corsaire Extraordinaire' from Marseilles, the exiled Captain who continued to sail in the service of the King?"

"Yes," said Blurtseau, "the very same."

"C'est un honeur," said Claude, crouching on one knee, "de faire votre conaissance."

Blurtseau embraced Claude, and Josette embraced Pableau, then Claude embraced Pableau, and Zurrabela embraced Josette, then Blurtseau, Pableau, and Claude embraced Zurrabela and

Josette, and when they had all finished embracing, they settled down to eat and fill in the spaces of their respective stories. After dinner, Claude let Pableau borrow his vielle á roue, and as the boulanger cranked out song after song, Zurrabela kept time on the castanets.

"Pableau makes a great baguette!"

"I only want what is best for France," said Blurtseau.
"What you want," said Zurrabela, "is a reality that can be

measured, a world that can be defined; not a process, but a paralysis."

"I want a consistent process," said Blurtseau, "one in which the principles of right and wrong are constant, and I can act with certainty."

"But that is not a process," said Zurrabela, "that's a closed sphere that excludes all that lies beyond it, an imaginary world that denies the world at large. In all the battles you fought, on land and at sea, did it never occur to you that the enemies you faced believed that they were as 'right' and 'justified' in their beliefs as you were in yours? If you look closely, you will see that the dynamic that once took place beyond the borders of France, is now taking place within."

"Yes," said Blurtseau, "I see that, but I can't tell which group is right, which group has the true interest of France at heart."

"That," said Zurrabela, "is for your countrymen to decide. It is the essence of democracy, and the responsibility that accompanies the future you seek. You can no longer be a follower, obeying as you would the lead of a king. Your country has set sail for a new world, a world whose challenges go beyond the question of national obedience, to the greatest challenge of all, that is, governing your self, coming to your own conclusions and acting on personal conviction. What is right? What is wrong? For France, for others, for me? These are the questions that each citizen must ask, the questions that your fellows are risking their lives to be able to ask."

"You were a sailor?" said Pableau.

"Yes," said Claude, "thirty-five years in the service of the Marine Nationale, pensioned with honor at the rank of vice-amiral d'escadre."

"Really?" said Zurrabela. "How exciting!"

"Yes," said Claude.

"Tell us about it," said Pableau.

"Yes," said Zurrabela, "tell us a story!"

"A story?" said Claude.

"Yes," said Zurrabela, "a story of danger and courage!"

"Hmm," said Claude, "well... I remember one time my ship was searching for pirates—Italian ships intercepting French sugar shipped from Haiti to Marseilles—and we were following a renegade schooner on its way to Civitavecchia, when suddenly, we were swallowed in a storm.

"'Lower the yard and reef the sail!' I cried to my first mate, Acajou Éduard, but my shout was drowned in the howl of the wind. We scrambled to reef the sail and fasten whatever could be fastened, but the wind rose from every quarter, lifting the sea mountain-high. Soon the ship was left to herself; now she climbed above the dark pit of hell, now she sank beneath the white peaks of heaven. Death was in every wave. Death was in every wave. Death was in every wave.

"A wall of water shattered the mast and we all had to scramble below deck. When we emerged, we found ourselves drifting in a cave whose darkness was more tangible than the dark from which we had escaped. After several hours, which seemed like several days, we emerged to a craterous lake, but found little cause to rejoice, for a noxious vapor rose from the lagoon and made respiration all but impossible.

"The lake's water was smooth and black, the only mark on its surface made by the splash of an occasional bird who, overcome by the fumes, plummeted to its death. Eventually, the fumes rendered the crew and myself unconscious and we drifted into a narrow, man-made canal. From there, we realized later, we continued to a smaller lake, down another canal, through the Gulf of Pozzuoli, and into the Gulf of Naples. As we came to our senses, a fishing barge missed us by the space of second, and the captain cried out as he passed, 'See Naples and die!'

"We sailed on, maneuvering as best we could through the crowded port, until we reached the open sea. From there we continued past the island of Capri, along the Amalfi coast, and on to the Gulf of Plicastro. As the sun began to set, Acajou attempted to repair the ship's steering, but before he could, we were swept into a small gorge. The passageway was announced by two enormous rocks, one of which reached majestically to the sky and whose peak was swallowed in a cloud. The mouth of a cave yawned from the middle of it, looking westward and turning toward the end of the earth.

"I stood in wonder, gazing at the magnificent peak, until my attention was called to a singular sight on my left. There, atop the cliffs, reclining in a verdant field, were nine women of incomparable beauty. They were surrounded by a scattering of human bones, and as they moved to the edge of the cliff, they sang with a voice of rare enchantment, 'Come, dear Captain, and hear our call. No man can sail past without bathing in the sweetness of our song, and he who listens will go away not only charmed, but wiser, for we know all there is to know.'

"I stood in rapture, listening to their song, and was about to run the ship aground, when suddenly a six-headed monster thrust its heads out of the overlooking cave. One of its mouths seized me by the waist and lifted me sprawling into the air, while the other five fell upon the singing sirens, crushing their bones with powerful jaws and tearing their skin with razor-sharp teeth. The head that had seized me soon went to join the others, dropping me in a heap on the foredeck, while the lovely throats of the sirens, which minutes before had given voice to the most enchanting of sounds, now rent the walls of the canyon with screams that shook the sky.

"Gasping, and coughing up blood, the victims were tossed to the sea where they stretched out their hands in agony to our departing ship. But our vessel sailed on, moving out of danger, and my first mate and I could only look in sorrow at the foaming water, stained with the spattering of blood. Several hours passed before we were able to speak, because we both knew we would never see a more horrible sight."

"These chantillies are delicious!" said Blurtseau.

"Enjoy them while you can," said Pableau, "they're the last ones I'll bake."

"What?!" said Blurtseau.

"Yes," said Zurrabela, "haven't you heard? The British have taken Haiti and cut off the French sugar supply."

"Can't you get it somewhere else?" said Josette.

"I'm afraid not," said Pableau, "90% of France's sugar is imported from Saint Domingue, that is, Haiti, and the fraction that now remains is taken directly to Paris."

"Quelle catastrophe!" cried Blurtseau.

"What can you do?" said Josette.

"Nothing," said Zurrabela, "except discontinue pastries and bake only baguettes."

"I've been thinking about your sugar problem," said Claude, "and I have an idea."

"Yes?" said Pableau.

"A friend of mine owns a fishing schooner, and he owes me a favor."

"A favor?" said Zurrabela.

"Yes," said Claude, "I saved his life in 1772, and he has agreed to lend me his boat for a short excursion."

"An excursion?" said Blurtseau.

"Yes," said Claude, "a sugar excursion."

"What do you mean?" said Pableau.

"As you may know," said Claude, "the British have been trying to befriend the Knights of Malta in order to gain an outpost in the Eastern Mediterranean, and they have been sending them shiploads of sugar and tea. The British ships depart from Gibraltar, skirt the North African coast, then cross to the coast of Italy, down to the Strait of Messina, and on to Malta. They sail within sight of land at all times, except when they cross from Africa to Italy, at which point they are momentarily vulnerable to a pirate attack."

"A pirate attack?" said Josette.

"Arrrrgghhhh," growled Blurtseau, "a pirate attack!"

"Arrrrgghhhh!" growled Pableau.

"Arrrrgghhhh!" growled Zurrabela.

"Arrrrgghhhh!" growled Claude, Josette, Blurtseau, Pableau and Zurrabela.

And so it was that the next day, as Zurrabela stayed behind to take care of the bakery and animals, Claude, Pableau, Josette and Blurtseau set sail, disguised as fishermen in search of a catch.

When they reached the point that Claude had calculated as the crossroads where they were certain to encounter the British frigate, he called for Blurtseau to drop anchor and for Pableau and Josette to prepare for the forthcoming delay. Blurtseau outlined a schedule of events designed to distract his fellows from dwelling upon the danger—and possible extinction—that lay ahead. He had engaged many a Man-of-War during his service to the decapitated king, and he admitted, if only to himself, that British sugar could cost dear. Claude, also, understood as much, and the two set about to entertain their companions in the manner that they had been entertained when, as young sailors, they had whiled away the hours before a life-threatening encounter.

Chief among the entertainments was song, and when Claude took it upon himself to teach Pableau the repertoire of sea chants that echoed in his brain, Pableau, with his unrivaled talent for imitation, performed them with such vigor and freshness that the listeners felt the songs had been improvised, right then and there, by the baritone baker. Blurtseau, for his part, continued his education of the enthusiastic Josette in the ways of ships and the sea, spending long hours teaching her the ropes—their magic and peril—as well as training her in the art of navigation, with its accompanying lessons in chart-reading and identification of the landmarks of the sky.

The waiting was, in fact, longer than either Claude or Blurtseau had anticipated, but the two captains and their crew, thanks in great part to the sumptuous array of pumpkin soups, pumpkin cakes, and pumpkin breads that issued from Pableau's kitchen, passed the time as merrily as ever they had on land, with the exception of the baker who, when rendering a sea-faring serenade, often shed a tear of yearning as he thought of his lonesome Zurrabela, peering out over the waves, anxiously awaiting her consort's return.

When the final store of sugar which Pableau had brought on board began to slip away like sands through a glass, the resolve of the shipmates was strengthened, and their individual differences—a peril for so many sailors before them—became woven together as four ropes are twined into one, until it seemed that the four were, and had been for the length of their days, a single mind, body, and soul. Even the dual command, built on mutual respect and whole-hearted veneration, proceeded without distress, to the point that when Claude began a sentence, Blurtseau would finish it, and vice versa, as if they had conjoined to share the breath necessary to furnish the information at hand, and when a question arose that required deliberation and decision, the resolution was reached in much the same way that one instrument in an orchestra takes up and finishes the motif suggested by another, enriching and enlivening the melody claimed by both.

Even at evening, as the four lounged lazily about the deck, and each one retreated to his or her individual self—Pableau to his thoughts of absent love, Josette to her exultation in the never-expected friendship around her, Blurtseau to memories of fond times with former crews under his command, and Claude, to the shadowy recollections of hope and horror in his youth, the vague memories that glowed for a moment in his mind, then vanished like smoke from his pipe—even then, as the sun began its ultimate descent to darkness, the two donkeys, the man, and the child—disengaged and dreamlike in the dusky stillness—inhaled and exhaled as one, silently bound together in the shimmering expanse of the sea.

"What are you doing?" said Josette.
"I'm sewing these pumpkins in an old fishnet," said Pableau, "so they won't roll around the deck."

"There she goes!" cried Blurtseau. "There! There! Off the port side! Harness the wind! Drop in behind! But at a distance!"

While Pableau and Josette fell to the sails, Claude took the wheel, and in no time the Zurabelle was riding in the wake of the British schooner. At evening, when the wind fell, the frigate came to rest and Claude dropped anchor behind.

"Ahoy there!" called a voice from the frigate. "State your business!"

"Ahoy!" cried Blurtseau in English. "Compatriots and comrades are we! And servants to her Majesty, trolling white water in search of a catch!"

"Very well!" cried the voice from the frigate. "But approach no further, lest you relish the taste of lead!"

Just before midnight a breeze began to blow, and Blurtseau and Pableau lowered a dory to the sea…

Moving with the speed of a lemur scrambling up a tree, Blurtseau swung a hook over the stern, scurried up the line, and vanished on the other side. In a trice he returned with a dozen sacks of sugar which he began to toss to Pableau, but when he went to toss the last sack, it slipped from his hoof and hit the sea with a splash. "Hey!" called a voice from the foredeck. "Who goes there?!"

"Curse these clumsy hoofs!" cried Blurtseau, leaping, goat-like, from the rear of the ship.

"Pull!" cried Blurtseau. "Pull! For the love of Poseidon! Pull!" Pableau put his back to the oars and the sugar-laden dory began to push its way through the waves. The crew of the frigate, now aware of the theft of their stores, scrambled to hoist sail and turn their lumbering craft in chase of the skiff. Blurtseau and Pableau continued to slice through the breakers, skipping after their schooner like a chick running after its mother.

By the time their dory had been raised and the sugar had been stowed, the Zurrabelle was swiftly under weigh, with the enemy in furious pursuit. Claude took the helm and Blurtseau scrambled up the rigging.

"The storm!" cried Blurtseau, spying a disturbance in the distance. "The storm! North by northeast! Sail for the storm! We'll lose 'em in the squall!"

Claude did as directed, with the British sloop behind, until pursuer and pursued were lost from sight beneath the watery peaks. Blurtseau, who could no longer see the enemy ship, turned to descend the rigging, but before he could, a wall of water struck the schooner, causing the hull to rock and roll, and throwing our hero—as if he had been pitched from a catapult—

into the frothing jaw of the sea. His companions watched in horror as he soared, head over hooves, describing a perfect parabola across the moonlit sky.

"Blurtseau!" called Pableau.

"Blurtseau!" called Josette.

"Blurtseau!" called Claude. But their comrade could not hear, or if he could, he could not reply, and the rudderless ship, steered now by the storm, drew quickly away, leaving our hero bobbing like a cork on the writhing water.

"We must turn and find him!" cried Pableau.

"But turn whither?" said Claude.

"Blurtseau is an excellent swimmer," said Pableau. "I'm sure he's secured a plank, or piece of driftwood, and is paddling for calmer seas. If we circle, describing a broader and broader circumference, we'll cross him with our bow."

"Yes," said Claude, "when the storm has settled."

And so they waited, tossed and turned in the belly of the gale, until the sky cleared. By dawn the British frigate, carried east with the careening clouds, was no longer to be seen, and the Zurrabelle was free to begin her search.

They sailed for fourteen days and fourteen nights, each day broadening the scope of their search, and each day encountering only sea. On the morning of the fifteenth day Pableau, perched on the foremast, thought he had spied his lost friend, but he was soon dismayed when closer inspection revealed a dark-grey dolphin. Josette, who had been holding up bravely, burst into tears, and Claude drew slowly and solemnly upon his pipe.

"It's time to head home," said Claude.

"What a thing it will be," said Pableau with false enthusiasm, "when we find that Blurtseau has been rescued, two weeks before, by a passing schooner, and that he and Zurrabela have been enjoying the days in Roquebrune, in happy anticipation of our return!"

The next morning Claude set their course for home, and the sails bellied out, white against the sky.

When they reached Roquebrune, and Blurtseau was not found, the survivors unhappily acknowledged the awful truth.

As time passed, Zurrabela filled in where Blurtseau had been, helping at the villa and overseeing Josette's education…

While Claude and Pableau sweat away their sorrow in the sun-drenched fatigue of harvest.

What are those papers? said Alex. That's my novel, said Blurtso. Your novel? said Alex. Yes, said Blurtso, *Blurtseau Lundif: Corsaire Extraordinaire*, would you like to hear it?

Sure, said Alex.. O.k., said Blurtso it goes like this, "… but their comrade could not hear, or if he could, he could not reply, and the rudderless ship, steered now by the storm, drew quickly away, leaving our hero bobbing like a cork on the writhing water." What? said Alex. "Leaving our hero bobbing like a cork," said Blurtso. I heard that, said Alex, but you can't kill your hero. I can't? said Blurtso. Of course not, said Alex. But he's lost at sea, said Blurtso. Then you'd better save him, said Alex. How? said Blurtso. I don't know, said Alex, maybe some kind of donkeus ex machina. Hmm, said Blurtso, donkeus ex machina…

"… but their comrade could not hear, or if he could, he could not reply, and the rudderless ship, steered now by the storm, drew quickly away, leaving our hero bobbing like a cork on the writhing water. Then suddenly…

"I'm saved! Pableau has thrown me a raft!"
And as the Zurrabelle disappeared in the distance, Blurtseau clung for life to his floating-gourd garden.

Blurtseau drifted through the sea and the stars... until he and his pumpkins finally found rest.

The beach where Blurtseau had landed was unforested and remote, and a week of wandering revealed he was on an island,

and that he was utterly alone. He quickly set about gathering any floating matter that might serve for a raft, but the island was ungenerous, and in a month he had still not fashioned a sea-worthy structure.

In truth, he was not entirely alone…

And as the days passed, Blurtseau made friends with the inhabitants of the island; the goats and grasshoppers and seals, the lizards and rabbits, the falcons, egrets, and gulls, and his favorites, the happy-go-lucky dolphins. It was a bountiful world. There was grass and myrtle, dozens of fresh-water pools, and countless alcoves to buffet the wind. The inhabitants went cheerfully about their business, finding whatever they desired. When he stopped dwelling on his future and past, Blurtseau delighted in watching them, scurrying and scampering about, and soon he joined in, playing games with goats, hopping with grasshoppers, and diving with dolphins...

Sometimes he would stand on a cliff...

And just let go... of form and substance and self... and become the wind... whipping the cliffs and tossing the clouds, gusting in canyons, chiseling stone, leaping and dashing and crashing, skipping with invisible hooves across the stretching claws of the sea.

Occasionally Blurtseau would spend an entire day watching the tides, and the next day he watched the clouds, or the motion of the goats on the hills, or the banter of the dolphins, or the flights and formations of the birds, and to Blurtseau it seemed a symphony, a polyphony of patterns, each one individual yet interacting, each one playing a part in other patterns, until it was all one pattern. And then he would  focus on a part, and the journey from microcosm to macrocosm would unfold anew.

Blurtseau, too, was a part of the pattern around him. His heart was a part, and his blood, and his lungs and his eyes and his ears. And every movement he made, every emotion, was as integral and essential as the land and the sea. But when his thoughts turned to the future, or the past, he would suddenly feel alone, and the impulse that had determined the course of his life—his search for fortune and fame, his blind search for what was already there—did not seem unreasonable or ill-guided at all.

 And when he felt alone, and needed a friend, he would turn to his imagination and say, "Look at those tracks, those hoofprints in the sand. They must be the tracks of my friend, my blurtseaugänger who has watched from afar, making sure I don't stumble and fall." And then he would say, "They are the tracks of my alter-

Blurtseau, the one who is never unhappy or sad. I'm sure he'll come, if I call, I'm sure he'll play, if I make up a game... One, two, three, four, five, six, seven... Here I come! Ready or not! Here I come!"

And off he would go, chasing the tracks of his invisible friend.

And sometimes he would think of his friends in Roquebrune…

One morning, when Blurtseau went for a swim…

He made an amazing discovery…

Would you look at that…

Wow!

Ahhhhhh…

. . . .

"Qui est elle?!"

Off he went, scurrying through the grass,
but when he emerged…

She was nowhere to be found.

"Where is she?" he thought. "Maybe she ran into the grass?" So he ran into the grass... and found only grass.

"Maybe she ran into the cave?" So he ran into the cave. "If I'm quiet I'll hear her hoofsteps. Yes! That's her! That's her clippety clop! Or is it only an echo... of my steps on the stone?"

When Blurtseau stopped, the echo stopped, and when he walked, the echo walked. "Yes," he concluded, "it's only an echo. Unless she's following me... walking and stopping, walking and stopping."

The days passed, and the weeks, and though he continued to search, poking his nose in every corner of the island, Blurtseau could not find the one he sought. Finally, he returned to the cave and the echo of his steps, and as he sauntered through the corridors he would bray, "Echo! Echo! Echo!" And the walls brayed back, "Echo! Echo! Echo!"

"Echo"

My heart casts an image in the night
that falls and spreads its light,
ripples silver and white,
leaves its image in the night.

The night casts an image in my mind
that falls and starts to unwind,
spreads and circles through time,
leaves its image in my mind.

My heart casts an image in the night
that echoes your name, Echo's your name.

My mind casts an image in my heart
that spreads and beats through every part,
falls and fills the dark,
leaves its image in my heart.

My mind casts an image in my heart
that echoes your name, Echo's your name.

I am an echo of the night,
an echo… of your name,
an echo… of your name.

My heart casts your name into the night,
your echo… casts your name into my mind,
your echo… casts your name into my heart,
you're Echo, Echo, Echo, Echo's your name.

My heart casts your name into the night… Echo.

The next day… Blurtseau heard hooves
that could not be his own.

"Hello," said Blurtseau.
"Hello," said Echo.
"I'm Blurtseau," said Blurtseau.
"Blurtseau," said Echo.
"What's your name?" said Blurtseau.
"Name?" said Echo.
"Yes," said Blurtseau, "what do you call yourself?"
"I don't call myself," said Echo.
"Can I call you Echo?" said Blurtseau.
"Echo?" said Echo.
"Yes," said Blurtseau, "Echo."

"How long have you been here?"
"I don't know," said Echo.
"Were you born here?"
"I don't think so,," said Echo.
"Maybe someone left you here."

"Is there really another world," said Echo, "beyond this?"

As the days passed, Blurtseau and Echo became friends.

And then... better friends.

Blurtseau told Echo about his life before the island — his voyages, the battles he had fought, the perils he had overcome — but though she listened with enthusiasm, she could scarcely imagine the things he described, for they were all things she had never seen. Bloodshed, of which there was much in his stories, was unknown on the island, and though she had witnessed aging in other animals — the goats in particular — the only deaths she had seen were the result of natural cause, and it seemed to her no more troubling than a deep and dreamless sleep. As for the humans, who commanded so much attention in his stories, she had never seen one, and could only picture them as hypercontentious goats walking upright. The towns and cities were unreservedly fantastic. She could not believe there were such things as streets and houses and palaces constructed from predetermined plans; a physical world built on the airy blueprints of imagination. She concluded that these magical creatures needed to do little more than imagine an object to make it appear, but she wondered why they chose to live in an artificial world rather than the real one that was already around them.

Blurtseau, for his part, found Echo's innocence to be as unimaginable as his lack of it, and he began to understand that what he saw, even the simplest object on the island, bore little resemblance to what she saw. And the meanings that he understood when he used the words he used were not the meanings she understood when she heard them. But he was enchanted by her innocence, and longed to know what it was like to live in her world, and she was content to play Desdemona to his Othello, losing herself in his tales, imbibing adventure as if slaking her thirst at a secret and mysterious spring.

As Blurtseau grew closer to Echo he began to consider how she would manage if they got off the island, if she were introduced to his world, and he feared she would be lost. She would be defenseless in a world of vanity, avarice and ambition, and the thought of leaving her behind made him sad. But whenever she saw he was sad, Echo would skip by with her cheerful clippety clop, and Blurtseau would forget his worries and join in whatever game she was playing. And how she did play!

Running, jumping, swimming—even the storms that passed by seemed to have been sent for her amusement, thrilling her with lightning pyrotechnics and rumbling symphonies of sound.

But Echo also began to consider what the future might hold. She had never felt lonely before Blurtseau arrived, and now the

island could not be fuller, but as she listened to the tales he told—tales of lovesick heroes and heroines suffering the struggle—it occurred to her that as easily as he had appeared, Blurtseau could disappear, and if he did, the island would not be the same one she had known before. She could not imagine not having met Blurtseau, and could not imagine a world without him, but she assured herself that he was exaggerating the sorrows of loneliness in his stories, and that the unpleasantness she might suffer upon his departure would be nothing compared to the joy of their time together.

With Echo near, Blurtseau was not lonely, but he was restless. The tales he had recounted made him think of his country. What was happening there? Had order been restored? Had the Lords of Grimaldi retaken Roquebrune? "If only I had some wood," said Blurtseau, "I could build a raft."

"Wood?" said Echo.

"It landed," said Echo, "a week before you arrived."

Echo recounted how she had come across the abandoned ship, but she had not seen any of the humans that Blurtseau had described. When they climbed aboard to see what was left inside, they found three barrels of flour, a treasure chest, and a dozen sacks of sugar.

When the goods were stored…

Blurtseau returned to the wreck and built a boat from the damaged wood and sails. "I've decided to take you with me," said Blurtseau, "when I leave tomorrow."

"What?" said Echo.

"I'm taking you to France," said Blurtseau.

"France?" said Echo.

"Yes," said Blurtseau, "and Roquebrune."

"I'm not going to France," said Echo.

"You're not?" said Blurtseau.

"No," said Echo.

"I thought you liked the stories I told," said Blurtseau, "all the descriptions of places and perils."

"Yes," said Echo, "they were very interesting, and I enjoyed them very much, but I'm not leaving the island."

"You're not?" said Blurtseau.

"No," said Echo.

"But what about adventure," said Blurtseau, "and the chance for fortune and fame?"

"I don't need fortune," said Echo, "I have everything I need right here."

"But what about fame," said Blurtseau, "don't you want people to know who you are?"

"As long as you know who I am," said Echo, "that's enough for me."

"But what about everyone else," said Blurtseau, "all the other animals and people in the world?"

"Why should I want them to know me?" said Echo.

"Because," said Blurtseau, "the more people that know and admire you, the happier you'll become."

"Really?" said Echo.

"Of course," said Blurtseau.

"Then why," said Echo, "are the people in your stories so anxious and yearning and sad?"

The next evening... Blurtseau set sail.

Believing his home lay eastward, he set his sails to a favorable wind, but as he sloshed through the sea he thought of Echo, and wondered if he was making an irreversible mistake.

Blurtseau sailed through the night and the day and the night, until he spied a beacon in the distance…

The next day, he walked to town...

Portofino, originally called "Portus Delphini" because of the unusual number of dolphins in the Tigullian Gulf, was a fishing village under the dominion of the Republic of Genoa.

Disguised as a fisherman,
Blurtseau slipped into the scenery.

In order to get the news of the day, Blurtseau lingered in the local tavern, and it was there he heard of a young soldier—born in Corsica to Genoese parents—who had recently been promoted to Captain in the French army. But the news, which a year before might have given cause for envy, scarcely held his attention, for his mind wandered, and he found himself daydreaming of Echo and their days on the island. Still, he was determined to reach Roquebrune, so he shook off his ennui and set to determining the safest route home, whether by land or by sea.

"What's that wonderful smell? It seems to be coming from the lighthouse."

"No, it's coming from in here…"

"What a nice patio…"

"And view."

"Gli ospiti arriveranno fra mezz'ora! Bring out the food!"

"How humiliating, to be used as a drink stand for fools like these... listen to them..."

"'Principessa' Maria Giuseppina, with her lackey husband, 'the future King of France.'"

"King of France?! King of thieves! King of assassins!"

"I'd rather be a Sardinian slave than King of the Franks!"

"A failed colony that won't outlast the century!"

"Cochons!" cried Blurtseau, leaping to the patio wall, "Écoutez-moi! Je suis Blurtseau L'un d'If, Corsaire Extraordinaire et Âne de la Montagne, fils e serviteur de mon cher pays, mon pays que n'a pas égal dans tout le monde! Vive la France! Vive l'honneur! Vive la belle Patrie!"

The group turned in stunned silence to the raving donkey, when one, realizing what he had heard, cried out, "It's Blurtseau Lundif! The Mediterranean marauder! Blood-thirsty pirate and anarchist legionnaire! Seize him! Seize him at once!"

In a moment the group was hurling curses and stones at the besieged captain who hopped and dodged atop the wall. With no escape in sight, Blurtseau seized the moment and…

Jumped.

Swimming for his life, Blurtseau paddled out to sea,
but his enemies were soon upon him and all seemed lost until…

A dolphin leapt to the rescue…

And carried him to Genoa.

With the Genoese patrolling the coast, Blurtseau fled inland until he reached Verona and the Republic of Venice.

Hoping the news of his flight had not preceded him…

He made his way to the center of town.

Later on, he stopped for a drink…

And made a new friend.

"I was born in Rome," said Francesco, "but moved to Florence at ten to work as a painter's apprentice. Later, I came to Verona, and now I rent boats and sell fish."

As the days passed and Blurtseau became comfortable with his new friend, he decided to trust him with the story of his flight from France. Francesco listened thoughtfully as Blurtseau recounted his tale of lost love and exile, and when he finished, Francesco sat for a moment in silence, then looked up from his wine and said, "I too have known love and loss, and have suffered political persecution."

Francesco went on to tell of how as a young apprentice in Florence, his master had been commissioned to paint the portrait of a local courtesan named Chiara Potinari, cousin of the generous Bandinelli family in Pisa. The painting, ordered by the prince of Medici, was to be unveiled at the engagement party of the courtesan and the prince. As apprentice, Francesco was to undertake the initial stages of the portrait, then turn it over to his master for the final touches. However, Francesco had scarcely begun when he fell violently in love with his ivory-skinned subject, and she likewise fell for him, and they decided to elope on the day the work was to be unveiled.

Fearing discovery in Florence, they fled to Verona and lived incogniti in a fisherman's hut on the river Adige. After several months, they were betrayed by an officer of the river patrol who noticed they did not rise with the other laborers, but lingered in the hut until late in the morning, and they sometimes did not rise until noon. He also remarked that they never had a thing to sell, and never made the trip to market.

As soon as Francesco and Chiara were called before the prefect, Chiara's identity was revealed and she was whisked away, while Francesco was taken to Florence and imprisoned in the royal dungeon. Twelve years later when he was released, he learned that Chiara had refused to marry the prince, and had taken her own life when she heard the false report that Francesco had been executed.

"You spent twelve years in the dungeon?"

"Yes," said Francesco, "and I would have surely expired, but a sympathetic prison guard brought me a collection of books, which enabled me to escape to my imagination."

"Wow," said Blurtso, "I was only in the dungeon at Versailles for three days, but it seemed like a lifetime!"

"A lifetime is what I lived," said Francesco, "as I had small hope of walking again in the light of day. But the moment came when the prince who had imprisoned me was trampled by a team of horses, and I was released to make room for enemies more dangerous than myself. The books I had read prepared me for my new life as architect, agronomist and inventor, and in three years I amassed a fortune."

Francesco went on to tell Blurtseau how he had opened a theatre company in Florence that performed the plays of Shakespeare in translation—translations that he himself had written—and he invested in the construction of an opera house in Milan called the "Nuovo Regio Ducale Teatro alla Scala," which became an instant success.

Blurtseau sat in wonder, listening to the extraordinary tale, but he did not ask why, after so much success, his friend now lived in a fisherman's hut on the Adige. He did ask, however, if

Francesco would be willing to suggest a course of study, for Blurtseau had come to realize he was not the Renaissance donkey he had believed he was, and that, except for expertise in battle and a few sentimental verses, he had not even begun to tap his infinite possibilities.

The days came and went, and the weeks and months, and despite the rigor of his studies, Blurtseau's mind wandered. In a real sense, he felt he was being torn in two. On one hand was his life as a warrior, defending his homeland and rising against injustice, and on the other was his growing love for culture and the arts, and for simple things. He reveled in the rhymed worlds of Dante and Petrarch, and the playful mischief of Boccaccio, and his thoughts often turned to Echo and the wisdom of her island. But it was too early to give up the physical rapture that had honed his body into a flawless fighting machine, a machine that fought without forethought, spontaneously parrying with a perfect balance of give and take. Yet now, had his instincts been altered? His equilibrium become unbalanced? Was he incapable of action without thought, without considering consequences beyond borders? Was this the price he paid for the loss of ignorance? For the joys of compassion? And as for his future, what did it mean? Fame and fortune now seemed empty next to a life of art, or a life of shared simplicity. Becoming a Renaissance donkey was not turning him into a harmonious whole, as he had hoped and expected, but was tearing him to pieces as the parts of himself vied, one against the others, for preeminence and control. And then there was his irrepressible sentimentality, as he continued to long for distant days with Pableau, Josette, and Echo.

"What?!" said Blurtseau.

"That's what I heard," said Francesco, "Napoleon's army is on the march."

"Do you think it's true?" said Blurtseau.

"I don't know," said Francesco.

"Wow," thought Blurtseau, "Napoleon!"

"What about Blurtsoiselle?" said Francesco.

"Blurtsoiselle?" said Blurtseau, "I don't think I'd recognize her if I saw her. My time with Echo has washed that away."

"Isn't it remarkable," said Francesco, "what a new love can do."

"Yes," said Blurtseau, "and what about Chiara, do you still miss her?"

"Yes," said Francesco, "that's why I live on the river, in the hut we shared."

"You never loved again?" said Blurtseau.

"No," said Francesco, "never."

"Your story has just begun," said Francesco, "and if you know where your heart lies, the battle is won."

"But Echo refused to come with me," said Blurtseau.

"A minor detail," said Francesco,
"that will be conquered the moment you see her again."

"It's true," said Blurtseau, "that I was never happier than

when I was on her island, but don't you think I'm too young to settle down?"

"Settle down?" said Francesco, "you won't settle down, your return will be the beginning of a new adventure. If she loves you the way you love her, and she assimilates your desires as you assimilate hers, she will long to know your world."

"And if she doesn't?" said Blurtseau.

"If she doesn't love you?" said Francesco.

"No," said Blurtseau, "if she doesn't long to know my world?"

"She will," said Francesco, "but you must give her time. Remember, she's never left the island. It was much easier for you to arrive than it will be for her to depart, and just as you don't want to abandon your world, she won't want to abandon hers. The adventure will be to chart a course between the two worlds, so that she will come to love yours as you have come to love hers. There will be decisions about particulars, to be sure, but the course of love, if it is true, will unfold naturally, though only if you are determined, inexorably determined, to stay together."

"Inexorably?" said Blurtseau.

"Yes," said Francesco, "inexorably."

"Once," said Blurtseau, "Echo and I swam with the dolphins!"

"Holy Corsica!" said Blurtseau. "Look at that horse!"

That's a great story, said Alex, but what happened to Echo?
Echo? said Blurtso.

While Blurtseau awaited Napoleon in Verona,
Echo came to a conclusion…

She could not live without her Corsaire Extraordinaire.

And so she set sail, without rudder, oars or sail, into the unimaginable unknown. And the days passed, and the nights, and the sea tossed her here, and the sea tossed her there, until she began to grow thirsty, and to despair... and with thirst and despair came fatigue, and with fatigue came a deep and dreamless sleep.

Unconscious and left for dead, fortune smiled on our hapless heroine...

But it was a cruel fortune...

Until the ship docked, and Echo was released...

With no idea where she was or how to get where she wanted to go, Echo began to walk. She remembered that Blurtseau had spoken of his friends in Roquebrune, and she reasoned that if she continued to walk along the coast, sooner or later she would come to the town, because while she had listened closely to the stories that Blurtseau had told, she had imagined that all the lands he spoke of were one land, a single island, only slightly bigger than her own, divided into parts called France, England, Italy, and the rest.

It had never occurred to her that no matter how long she walked around England, she would never get to France.

As she walked, the wind began to rise and Echo turned inland. Then it started to rain, not downwards, but sideways, pelting and piercing her skin. She stopped in her tracks. Should she return to the port, or continue the direction she was going? And what direction was that? North, south, east, west? The wind thundered in her ears and the rain stung her eyes. She realized that she would have to do something if she didn't want to expire, so she continued inland, following the line of a low stone wall.

The wind-blown grass sliced her ankles and shins as she walked, and she closed her eyes. She knew that some living creature had built that wall, and that by following it she might find that creature, and that creature might have a shelter where she could take refuge. She walked and walked and walked and walked, until her hooves grew weary and her haunches cramped, and her body shivered with cold. But still she continued, feeling her way along the wall, occasionally scraping her shoulder on an ill-placed stone.

She tried to think of happier times, playing on her island, splashing in the waves that rolled to the shore, but her efforts were in vain, for the shivers that racked her body racked her mind as well. Finally, with no strength to continue, she dropped to her knees and nestled into the grass at the base of the wall.

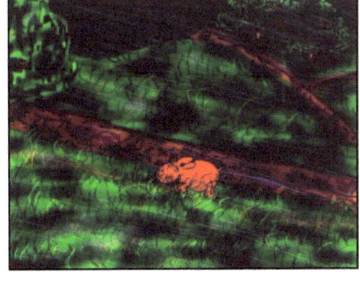

Delirious with fatigue, Echo remained there, sheltered by the wall and grasses, resigned to the idea that this would be her final resting place, that her life had been an unawakened dream until the day she left her island to awake to the nightmare that was now around her. She had awakened, but only in time to sleep once and for all, because she was a creature born to live in only one element, and once removed was doomed to extinction. As she lay there shivering, waiting for the death that could not be worse than the life she was living, she slipped into a calm and eventless sleep.

And she slept, breathing in short, shallow puffs, and the hours passed, and the storm passed, and the night passed, and the slow rising sun finally peeked over the horizon and warmed the air, and ground, and grasses. And as the grasses warmed, Echo warmed as well, and her breathing became slower, deeper, and more even, but still she slept, and slept and slept and slept, until before she could understand what was happening, not knowing where she was or how she had come there, a damp, warm snout pressed against her ear, and she jumped up with a start.

Uncertain on her hooves, she teetered, bracing herself against the wall, then opened her eyes to focus on a squat, pink figure standing on four legs in front of her.

"What kind of animal are you?" said Echo.
"I'm a pig," said Winston.
"A pig?" said Echo.

"Yes," said Winston, "a pig."

"I'm a donkey," said Echo.

"Yes," said Winston, "I know, there are donkeys in many parts of England."

"England?" said Echo.

"Yes," said Winston.

"Is England far from France?" said Echo.

"No," said Winston, "France is just across the water."

"The water?" said Echo.

"Yes," said Winston.

"Is it close enough to swim?" said Echo.

"No," said Winston, "you have to take a boat."

"Do you have a boat?" said Echo.

"No," said Winston.

"Oh," said Echo.

Echo was fatigued from her night in the storm, and after a few more questions about France, she asked Winston if there was a safe place to rest. Winston replied she could rest in the stable of his master's house, which was just down the road. He explained that his master had gone to London for the week, and had taken his horse, so she could have her run of the yard.

"Feeling better?" said Winston.

"Yes," said Echo, "I had a lovely nap, and the grass is very comfortable."

"My straw is your straw," said Winston.

"The master won't mind," said Echo, "if he finds it tossed around the stable?"

"No," said Winston, "we can eat it before then."

"Tell me about France," said Echo.

"France," said Winston, "is the most thrilling place in the world, but it's very dangerous. There are wild animals that prowl the fields, and humans that speak a language no one understands."

"What language is that?" said Echo.

"French," said Winston.

"What language do people speak here?" said Echo.

"English," said Winston.

"What's the difference?" said Echo.

"English," said Winston, "is spoken by civilized people, and French is spoken by barbarians."

"Civilized people?" said Echo.

"Yes," said Winston, "people who don't kill each other for a loaf of bread."

"What's a loaf of bread?"

"A loaf of bread is something humans eat after they cook it in an oven heated by fire… it's like straw for donkeys."

"And the French," said Echo, "kill each other to get it?"

"Yes," said Winston, "they had a revolution because the queen told them to eat cake instead of bread."

"What's a revolution?" said Echo.

"A revolution is when a lot of people who don't have bread kill a lot of people who do."

"Bread must be very tasty," said Echo.

"Personally," said Winston, "I prefer roots and flowers, but humans are odd."

"What else do the French do?" said Echo.

"Well," said Winston, "I've heard they're still hungry from the revolution, and now they want English bread… there's even a general named Napoleon who wants to eat all the bread in the world."

"All the bread in the world?" said Echo.

"Yes," said Winston.

"How big is the world?" said Echo.

"Very big," said Winston.

"How big?" said Echo.

"Bigger than this stable," said Winston.

"That's not so big," said Echo.

"It depends on how much bigger," said Winston.

"I have a friend from France," said Echo, "who talked a lot about sugar, but never mentioned bread."

"Sugar is important too," said Winston.

"Why?" said Echo.

"Because people put it in their tea," said Winston.

"Their tea?" said Echo.

"Yes," said Winston, "a drink made from leaves and water heated by fire."

"Do humans use fire for everything?" said Echo.

"Yes," said Winston, "most everything."

"That's interesting," said Echo. "What is fire?"

As Winston continued to enumerate the barbarous habits of France, and the civilized traditions of England, Echo began to realize that the search she had undertaken would not be easy, for in order to survive she would have to understand the geography, politics, and idiosyncratic customs of each one of the lands she visited. Fortunately, there was Winston, who in addition to having a generous and affectionate heart, clearly knew everything about everything.

"Is this the water I cross to get to France?" said Echo.
"No," said Winston, "you have to leave from Dover."
"I landed at Dover," said Echo.
"Yes," said Winston, "many ships land there."
"The cliffs are striking," said Echo.
"Are they?" said Winston.
"You haven't seen them?" said Echo.
"No," said Winston.
"How did you get to France?" said Echo.
"I've never been to France," said Winston.
"Really?" said Echo.
"Really," said Winston.
"Where have you been?" said Echo.
"I've never been anywhere," said Winston.
"Not anywhere?" said Echo.

"Well," said Winston, "there's a town down the road called Ashton."

"Have you been there?" said Echo.

"No," said Winston.

"Would you like to go?" said Echo.

"No," said Winston.

"How about going to France?" said Echo.

"Not on your life," said Winston.

Echo was more than a little disappointed to find her friend had only heard of the places he talked about, and had never actually been there, but she still valued his knowledge, because he knew more than she did, and she set about to convince him to join her in her search.

"Roquebrune?" said Winston. "No, I've never heard of it."

"It's on the coast of France," said Echo.

"Across from Dover?"

"Yes," said Echo.

"What's so special about Roquebrune?" said Winston.

"It's the pig capital of the world," said Echo.

"It is?" said Winston.

"Yes," said Echo, "it's the only place on earth where pigs rule and humans do their bidding."

"Really?" said Winston, "strange I've never heard of it."

"Humans don't want you to hear of it," said Echo, "because they're afraid you'll run away to live there."

"You know," said Winston, "I've never completely trusted humans, even my master who makes sure I've got plenty to eat, sometimes has a strange hunger in his eyes."

"In Roquebrune," said Echo, "you could be your own master, and maybe even be a governor or king."

"A king?" said Winston.

"Sure," said Echo.

"Hmm," said Winston, "I wonder if I'd be a good king?"

"Of course you would."

"And the humans would call me 'My Lord'?" said Winston.

"They'd have to," said Echo.

"How do you know so much about Roquebrune?" said Winston.

"My friend told me about it," said Echo, "my friend Blurtseau Lundif."

"Is Blurtseau a pig?" said Winston.

"No," said Echo, "he's a donkey, but he likes pigs."

"Hmm," said Winston, "'Lord Winston' has a nice ring to it."

"It certainly does," said Echo.

Echo spent a fitful and sleepless night. She had never told a lie before—she didn't know what a lie was—and she felt terrible about the things she had said. Of course, she didn't know for sure those things weren't true, pigs may well be the rulers of Roquebrune, for though she remembered Blurtseau talking about the Prince of Monaco, who was a human, and the King of France, she had never  heard him mention the King of Roquebrune. And after all,

Winston would make a fine king, maybe the best king that ever was. But still, she knew in her heart she had deceived her friend, and she vowed to confess her deception the first chance she got.

"I have a confession," said Echo.

"A confession?" said Winston.

"Yes," said Echo, "I'm not sure if Roquebrune is ruled by pigs."

"It's not?" said Winston.

"I don't know," said Echo.

"No pig governor?" said Winston. "No pig king?"

"I don't know," said Echo, "my friend who lived there said a town nearby is ruled by humans."

"Did he say Roquebrune was ruled by humans?"

"No," said Echo, "but he didn't say it was ruled by pigs."

"But it might be ruled by pigs?"

"Yes," said Echo, "it might, but it probably isn't."

"Why not?" said Winston.

"Because everywhere else," said Echo, "seems to be ruled by humans."

"That's true," said Winston, "but it doesn't mean there's not a town somewhere that's ruled by pigs."

"That's true," said Echo.

"And," said Winston, "that town might be Roquebrune."

"Yes," said Echo, "it might."

"And even if Roquebrune is currently ruled by humans," said Winston, "the pigs in town might rise up one day and seize control."

"Yes," said Echo, "they might."

"And maybe," said Winston, "they're just waiting for a special pig to lead them, and that pig might be me."

"Yes," said Echo, "it might."

"So," said Winston, "what did you want to confess?"

"I wanted to confess," said Echo, "that I don't know."

"That's o.k.," said Winston, "there are some things that even I don't know."

"What are you doing?" said Echo.

"I'm reading," said Winston.

"Reading?" said Echo.

"Yes," said Winston, "I'm reading *Demeter's Manual of Parliamentary Law and Procedure*. Would you like to hear what it says?"

"What do you mean hear what it says?" said Echo.

"What the book says," said Winston.

"The book can talk?" said Echo.

"No," said Winston, "not by itself, but it can when someone reads it."

"What do you mean?" said Echo.

"Humans," said Winston, "write the words they use when they talk on the pages of books so they can talk to people who aren't there, and so the people who read them can listen to people who aren't there."

"That's incredible," said Echo.

"Yes," said Winston.

"Who is talking through that book?" said Echo.

"A person who knows everything there is to know about Parliamentary Law," said Winston.

"Parliamentary Law?" said Echo.

"The Parliament," said Winston, "is a group of humans who make all the laws in England, and this book describes the procedure of making those laws."

"The laws?" said Echo.

"Yes," said Winston, "the rules humans live by so they don't kill each other for a loaf of bread."

"Civilization!" said Echo.

"Exactly," said Winston.

"How many laws does England have?" said Echo.

"Thousands and thousands," said Winston.

"Why so many?" said Echo.

"Because," said Winston, "humans need a lot of civilizing."

"Do donkeys and pigs have a book of laws?" said Echo.

"No," said Winston, "we're already civilized."

"Why are you reading about Parliamentary Law," said Echo, "if pigs don't need laws?"

"Because," said Winston, "when I become the King of Roquebrune, the humans under my control will still need guidance."

"Oh," said Echo, "you mean new laws?"

"Yes," said Winston.

"Like what?" said Echo.

"Well," said Winston, "to begin with I'll outlaw bread."

"Bread?" said Echo.

"Yes," said Winston, "so they won't want to kill each other."

"That's wise," said Echo.

"Thank you," said Winston.

"What about pastries?" said Echo.

"Pastries?" said Winston.

"Yes," said Echo, "Blurtseau told me his friend Pableau made the most delicious pastries."

"Like what?" said Winston.

"I think he called them 'petits choux chantillies,'" said Echo.

"I've never heard of that," said Winston, "what is it?"

"I don't know," said Echo, "but he said they were good to eat and he had to steal some sugar to make them."

"Steal some sugar?" said Winston.

"Yes," said Echo, "Blurtseau and his friends attacked a British ship carrying sugar and tea to Malta, but on the way home he was washed overboard and had to save himself by clinging to a raft of pumpkins. That's how he reached my island."

"He attacked a British ship?!" said Winston.

"Yes," said Echo, "I believe it was British, but it might have been French."

"It must have been French," said Winston, "a British ship would never let itself be attacked."

"Of course not," said Echo, "it must have been French."

"At any rate," said Winston, "sugar is as bad as bread, so I'll outlaw it as well."

"I don't know," said Echo, "it sounds like you're going to have to outlaw everything that people want."

"Yes," said Winston, "it sounds that way."

"That's just silly," said Echo.

"Maybe," said Winston, "being the king of Roquebrune will be harder than I thought."

"Yes," said Echo, "if you want to be a good king."

"If I can't be a good king," said Winston, "I don't want to be a king at all."

"I don't blame you," said Echo.

"It occurs to me," said Winston, "that if I found out what makes a person good, I could make good laws and be a good king."

"That would be reasonable," said Echo.

"What do you think," said Winston, "makes a person good?"

"I'm not sure," said Echo, "I don't know any people."

"Well," said Winston, "what makes a donkey good?"

"I don't know that either," said Echo, "I've only met one donkey other than myself."

"Blurtseau Lundif?" said Winston.

"Yes," said Echo.

"Was he a good donkey?" said Winston.

"Yes," said Echo.

"Maybe," said Winston, "we're going about this the wrong way… maybe we should consider what makes a person bad, then do the opposite to make them good."

"That makes sense," said Echo.

"O.k.," said Winston, "what makes a person bad?"

"Bread?" said Echo.

"Yes," said Winston, "but why does it make them bad?"

"Because they want it when they don't have it," said Echo.

"Yes," said Winston, "and why do they want it?"

"Because they like to eat it," said Echo.

"Yes," said Winston, "but donkeys like to eat grass, and grass doesn't make them bad."

"That's because they almost always have it," said Echo.

"Yes," said Winston, "but not all donkeys are satisfied with grass."

"They're not?" said Echo.

"No," said Winston, "you said Blurtseau Lundif attacked a ship because he wanted sugar for his pastries."

"Yes he did," said Echo, "and then he left my island because he wasn't satisfied there."

"Were you satisfied there?" said Winston.

"Yes," said Echo, "until Blurtseau left, and I started to miss him."

"So," said Winston, "you were satisfied before he arrived, and you were satisfied when he was there, but you were not satisfied when he left?"

"Yes," said Echo.

"And Blurtseau," said Winston, "was probably satisfied with grass before pastries, but he wasn't satisfied after."

"Yes," said Echo.

"I think we're on to something," said Winston.

"Really?" said Echo.

"Yes," said Winston, "something about the importance of being satisfied with what you already have."

"Yes," said Echo, "but what if a person doesn't already have bread?"

"Then they should be satisfied with something they do have," said Winston.

"What if they don't have anything?" said Echo.

"Anything to eat?" said Winston.

"Yes," said Echo.

"Maybe the problem with people," said Winston, "is that they can't eat grass."

"Yes," said Echo, "but do you think they'd be satisfied with grass?"

"Probably not," said Winston.

"Maybe the problem," said Echo, "is that people can't be satisfied with anything."

"Now," said Winston, "we're getting somewhere!"

One day Winston took Echo to visit Ashton. It was Echo's first time in a town, for she had not entered Dover upon disembarking, and she was amazed to see that everything was as Blurtseau had said it would be... there were streets and houses and shops, and humans at every turn walking on their hind legs, and vehicles on something called wheels, pulled by overgrown donkeys called horses. It was really quite pleasant, she had to admit, for even the ugliest buildings were decorated with flowers beneath the windows and ornaments on the doors. And so they walked, chattering as they went, until suddenly upon turning a corner, a hand reached out, seized Winston by the throat, and whisked him into a shop.

Echo stood there, dumbfounded in the street, not knowing what to do or why someone would accost her friend, when presently, from inside the shop, a blood-curdling squeal pierced her ears. Moments later a human emerged with a rag, wiping a sticky red liquid from his hands. Instantly, all the gruesome stories Echo had heard about humans flashed through her mind. Unable to move, she watched as the butcher returned to his shop and hung the left flank of Winston from a hook in the window.

Echo remained in the street until the sun set and the people returned to their homes. A fire had been ignited within her, a cold fire sparked by disbelief, fueled by horror, and fanned by rage. And the fire grew, minute by minute, with each quickening breath and blink of her eyes that opened to the sight of her slaughtered friend, until finally, without warning, it exploded in a blaze of motion and she kicked down the door and roared into the shop.

Echo was here, she was there, she was here, there, there, here, kicking, diving, demolishing everything in reach until suddenly, out of the corner of her ear, she heard a muffled cry…

"Winston!" said Echo.
"You're not dead!"

"No," said Winston, "the butcher put me in this sack before he slaughtered the pig in the window."

"Let's go away," said Winston. "To France?" said Echo. "Yes," said Winston, "to the city of pigs."

At Dover, they looked for a way to cross the channel.

Using some old crates, they disguised themselves and stowed away.

But once they reached France, they encountered a problem...

"No," said Winston, "I don't speak French."

At the same time, Blurtseau, hoping to entreat Napoleon to rule Verona with respect and compassion, made his way to Paris, leaving Italy for his beloved France.

"Is that Paris up ahead?" said Echo.

"No," said Winston, "I don't think so, Paris is supposed to be pretty big."

"Bigger than Ashford and Dover?" said Echo.

"No," said Winston, "not that big."

"When I reach Notre Dame," thought Blurtseau, "I can lose myself in the crowd."

Meanwhile, in Menton, Pableau found a familiar face…

"Blurtsoiselle?"

"No sooner had I run off with the cousin of the King," said Blurtsoiselle, "than he abandoned me at a roadside inn on the way to Versailles. I found my way back to Paris, but by the time I arrived, the capital was in chaos and I was abducted and put to work pulling carts carrying the dead to mass graves on the outskirts of town. After six months of laboring from dawn until dusk, with little to eat, I became too weak to pull the carts, and was left to die in one of the graves. The  robbers who pillaged the site, looking for anything of value—a pair of shoes, a threadbare shirt, a gold filling—found me alive among the carrion and took me to the catacombs beneath the city. When I realized they intended to kill and eat me, I escaped into a sewer where I lived on the city's dregs, until I emerged from a chute that emptied into the Seine.

"For the next three years I lived under the Pont Neuf, scavenging for the crumbs left by the faithful going to and from Notre Dame, until one day, I met a man who was moving to Nice, and offered to pull his wagon to the coast if he would feed me along the way. When we arrived in Nice, he had no more use for me, so I continued to Roquebrune where I searched for Blurtseau, and when I didn't find him, I came to Menton, where I found a job weaving funeral wreathes."

"Blurtseau?" said Pableau. "He was lost at sea, and we have been forced to go on without him. But time passes, and Zurrabela and I are grateful for what we have—our two dear friends Claude and Josette, our bakery, and each other."

"I think I'll take some chantillies to Blutsoiselle tomorrow," said Zurrabela.

"That's a good idea," said Pableau, "it might cheer her up."

"Can you teach me to paint?" said Josette.
"Sure," said Zurrabela.

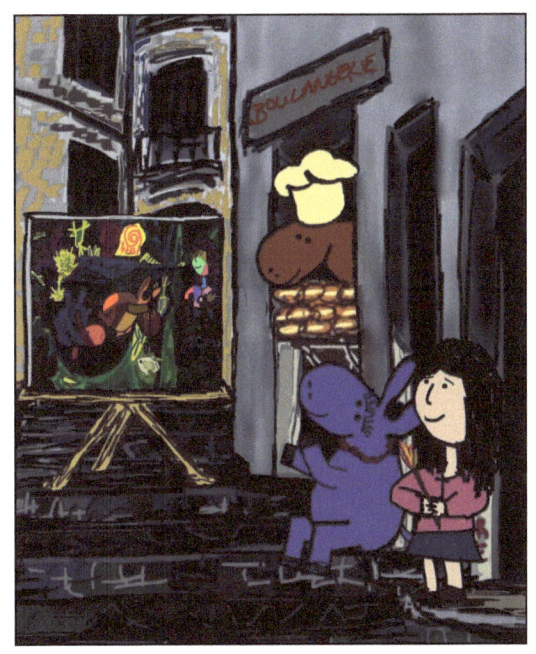

"I like it," said Pableau. "Why don't you sell your paintings in Menton?"

"Pableau cherche des poissons"

"Mme la Fourchette mange son éclair"

"Deux baguettes et seulement un chat"

"Pableau attend Zurrabelle"

"Zurrabelle cherche des oeufs"

"Une promenade dans la ville"

"La Boulangerie"

"Claire d'âne"

"Josette peint Zurrabelle"

"Le beveur de cacao"

"La fontaine de Roquebrune"

"Plongeurs à Saint Raphael"

"En nageant à Antibes"

"Mme la Fourchette poursuit les oiseaux"

"Mme la Fourchette nettoie les tapis"

"Can you believe it," said Zurrabela, "Honoré IV, Prince of Monaco, has offered 10,000 francs for this painting."

"10,000 francs!" said Pableau, "that's not possible!"

"Yes," said Zurrabela, "we met him yesterday in Menton, and he's sending someone for the painting today."

"What will you do with the all that money?" said Pableau.

"I'm going to buy the villa where we've been working," said Josette.

While Josette painted, the rest settled into their new home, determined to make the best use of their time.

The arching wave expires, gives way
to the hollow of the next day behind.
Meandering days like the sea in calm
spurning the storm.
Broken spray that's forgotten
the journey of pull and hollow and swell.

The seabirds don't reach the city,
caught on the currents rising:
the waves, the breath,
the aroma of equinox.

The city sinks,
absorbed in itself,
lost in the reflection
of shadow and sky.

The tide, the world, the day,
release their grip,
career to their center
beneath the slippery back of the sea.

The villa was large enough that, for the first time, Josette was given her own room, but the gift did not bring pleasure, for she had become accustomed to the breathing of her friends as they had all slept in their one-room cottage, and she was unsettled by the strange silence. As a result, she did not enjoy a single moment of slumber in any of the first three  nights in her new bed. On the fourth night, as she was staring hopelessly at the ceiling beams and watching the moving shadows cast by the leaves outside her window, she heard a thump at the door.

The sound, which began softly, soon became more pronounced, until the door slowly opened, but no figure appeared.  Terrified, Josette stretched out stiff and breathless, until she heard the clicking of little hooves moving across the floor... It was one of the pigs! Josette let out a sigh as she watched the pink mass make its way to the foot of the bed and settle down to sleep. With the rhythm of her friend's exhalations, Josette began to relax, and in no time she slipped into a deep and restful sleep.

Meanwhile, in Paris, Blurtseau waited for an audience with

Napoleon, but as power always comes to fear power, Blurtseau soon discovered that Napoleon was as threatened by Blurtseau's popularity as the King had been before.

"Allez debout! Saisissez le Corsaire!"

And so it was that once again Blurtseau Lundif, Corsaire Extraordinaire, Âne de la Montagne, and BlurtZo de la Brava Espada, fled Paris, returning to the only place he had ever found peace... Roquebrune and the Côte d'Azur.

In another part of Paris...

"It's hard to believe," said Winston, "this wasn't built by the British."

As Winston and Echo made their way through the streets of Paris, they began to feel more and more uneasy. They had never imagined there were so many people in the world. Everywhere they turned, they saw larger and larger crowds, parades of feet hurrying to some urgent destination, and every one of them was speaking a language neither Echo nor Winston could understand. The only word they knew was the name of the town where Blurtseau had lived, Roquebrune. And so, hoping someone might recognize the town and point them in the proper direction, they stood on a corner repeating that single word, "Roquebrune? Roquebrune? Roquebrune?"

Of course, it was highly unlikely that any of the passersby would recognize the name of a town of 500 inhabitants, 400 kilometers to the south; a principality that had just become a part of

France. As a result, Echo's and Winston's inquiries elicited nothing more than puzzled looks and an occasional hungry glance, a glance that made Winston tremble, remembering his nightmarish experience in the Butcher's Shop. Echo, too, was frightened by the things she saw, and by the din of sounds that thundered in her ears. She looked to Winston for courage, and though her friend was as panicked as she, his innate sense of self-importance, and belief he knew everything, enabled him to move confidently forward, repeating with every stride, "Roquebrune? Roquebrune? Roquebrune?"

By the end of their first day, Echo and Winston were exhausted and hungry. Though they had passed shops selling all types of food, and humans constantly engaged in the act of eating—even while they walked—Echo and Winston had not stumbled across a single discarded crumb until they chanced upon a plaza where a farmer's market was being disassembled. They stuffed themselves with carrot tops and brown lettuce until they were full, and when it began to rain they walked down to a wide green river and took shelter under an enormous stone bridge.

As soon as Blurtseau reached Monaco,
he started for Roquebrune.

"I wonder," thought Blurtseau, "if Pableau and the others survived the storm, or if I'm walking into an empty grave?"

"It looks abandoned…

I guess they didn't make it."

Gone... Blurtseau had never truly considered a world without his friend Pableau. He had imagined life apart from him, receiving an occasional epistle relating his whereabouts—he had never expected him to remain forever in Roquebrune—but his demise, a world without him, that was an unimaginable world, inexorably foreign and empty.

The abandoned cottage was as he had remembered, and it was clear no other residents had ventured in. "A world without friends," he thought. "I suppose I could return to Verona."

Suddenly the image of Echo, alone on her island, pierced him like an arrow. She had been right, and he had been wrong. There was no past to go back to, and no future of fame and fortune. There was only the prison of the present, this empty night he had chosen over the Eden of Echo's island.

He considered what she would have suffered had she come with him, how unsuited she would be for the peopled planet, a planet where past is piled upon past, until no stone remains untrod. When night had fully fallen, and the earth and trees lay still beneath the waning moon, Blurtseau took a final turn around the yard, looking for any sign of promise, but finding none, he returned to the fire, hoping its heat would warm at least the fringes of the unsoundable space inside him.

As the weeks passed, Blurtseau spent his days walking up and down the coast, searching for any vestige of his lost life.

Though his friends were not to be found, and his spirit was sullen and morose, he noticed that while he walked he would occasionally be seized with a sensation of joy. A moment, passing as quickly as it came, marked by a specific sensory experience.

The first time it happened he was walking the familiar path from Menton to Roquebrune, noticing a stone he had not noticed before, a stone he had passed more than a hundred times, when suddenly from the lump of granite Josette's voice rang out as if she were walking at his side. And with each word of the seemingly insignificant phrase she uttered, Blurtseau was speared with a flash of time beyond time, as if a bell had been struck inside him. But then it was gone—the phrase, the vibration, the transformation—and once again the coast and alleys were empty and abandoned, except for the sound of himself, clippety cloppeting up and down, over and around, here and there, searching for a glimmer of his vanquished past.

Some days would pass without the hint of a recollection, until suddenly the echo of Blurtseau's hooves in an alley would bring the vision of a cave on Echo's island, the rhythm of her breath, and the warmth of her muzzle against him.

And the next moment the pattern of a shadow, or the breeze with its mixture of moisture and warmth, would bring the image of Pableau, grazing in the grass, or planting pumpkins in the yard. And then came the kaleidoscope of smells, the fragrance of a flower, the scent of eucalyptus, the afternoon aromas of cooking and their companion sounds, clinking silverware, voices calling family to table, shoes slapping on stone, and eyes and smiles in the windows.

And some days Blurtseau would just sit, watching the people climb and descend, until it was time to walk home, following the same alleys and lanes that Pableau and Zurrabela had followed after a day at the bakery.

Back at the cottage, as evening waxed and the birds twittered farewell to the day, he would pause at the door, lingering in the last tones of twilight, then go in to prepare the evening's fire. And as the flames cast shadows on the walls and beams of the cottage, he would remember the light of sunset in Echo's cave, how it glowed above the majestic dome, and he would remem-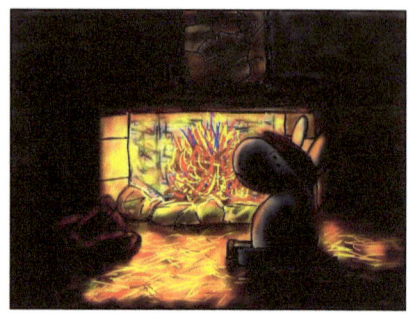ber the intelligent and innocent conversations they shared before dozing off, and how they would sleep soundly until the first birds peeked in above. He remembered how the dust particles would hang in the morning rays that illuminated the opposite wall, and how the light would descend, filling and warming the shadowy air.

And so the days passed, until…

"Is that pound cake I smell?"

While Blurtseau mourned what he believed lost, his friends enjoyed the villa, though they faced a familiar challenge.

"Do you think we should reopen the bakery?" said Zurrabela.

"Yes," said Pableau, "but we'll have to ration the remaining sugar."

"How much is left?" said Zurrabela.

"I think we have enough to bake pastries two days a week for six months."

"And then?" said Zurrabela.

"Then we'll have to get more," said Pableau.

"Oh no!" said Zurrabela, "You won't go back to sea!"

"No," said Pableau, "I'm going to plant beets."

"Beets?" said Zurrabela.

"Yes," said Pableau, "sugar beets. I met a neighbor who's making sugar by boiling and straining the juice."

"Really?" said Zurrabela.

"Yes," said Pableau, "we can grow them on the land below the cottage. If we seed the entire space, we'll have enough sugar to bake two days a week for a year."

"When will you start planting?" said Zurrabela.

"I'll clear the field tomorrow and plow the day after."

I like it, said Alex, but there seems to be something missing. Missing? said Blurtso. Yes, said Alex, there's no villain. Every great novel needs a great villain, a counterpart to the hero, a mirror from the other side. Hmmm, said Blurtso, a villain....

"Doctor Arlan de Borneo," said Lord Alecs. "I'm so pleased you could join us."

"At your service," my Lord.

"I've made room for your quarters," said Lord Alecs, "by reducing the number of crew. You'll have to fill in wherever you're needed."

"Aye, aye, Captain."

"Death to Napoleon!" growled Alecs. "And death to Blurtseau Lundif! The sugar-stealing marauder wrapped in French rags!"

"Why are there so many statues of people nailed to trees?" said Echo.

"Nailed to trees?" said Winston.

"Yes," said Echo, "trees made of crossed sticks."

"Oh," said Winston, "that's Jesus Christ."

"Jesus Christ?" said Echo.

"Yes," said Winston, "he was killed, and after he died they nailed him to a cross."

"Wow," said Echo, "he must have stolen a lot of bread!"

"No," said Winston, "he tried to convince people to live simple, loving lives."

"Like donkeys and pigs?" said Echo.

"Exactly," said Winston.

"It doesn't look like he convinced many people," said Echo."

"No," said Winston, "but a few of them took it to heart. They're just hard to spot, because they're not the ones trying to be noticed."

After a week in Paris, Echo and Winston had made no progress toward their ultimate destination, and when it became clear that none of the humans had ever heard of Roquebrune, Winston hit upon a new plan—they might recognize the name, "Blurtseau Lundif." So he and Echo began saying "Blurtseau Lundif" instead of "Roquebrune" to each person who passed.

In no time they got a bite. A man wearing some sort of uniform stopped and repeated, "Blurtseau Lundif?" To which Winston nodded and replied, "Blurtseau Lundif."

"Blurtseau Lundif?" said the man."Le Corsaire Extraordinaire de Marseilles?"

"Marseilles?" repeated Winston.

"Oui, oui," said the man, "Marseilles."

"Marseilles?" said Winston, pointing his snout to the north.

"Non, non," said the man, pointing to the south. And so it was that Winston and Echo made their way out of Paris and took the first road south.

As the days passed, Winston and Echo walked on, asking each person they met, "Marseilles?", and slowly but surely coming closer and closer to the bustling sea port where Blurtseau had been raised, and from where he had set sail countless times with his faithful crew.

It had been a relief to emerge from the chaos and noise of Paris, and Echo was pleased to see the rolling hills and valleys, and to meet the friendly, hard-working people. Winston, too, had to admit that the French were not the monsters he had believed them to be, though he was wary of the hungry look in their eyes. Of course, they talked as they walked, or rather Winston talked and Echo listened, and the familiar prattle made Echo feel certain that no matter where they were, or what obstacles they encountered, everything would eventually work out; Winston would find his city of pigs, and she would find her Blurtseau Lundif.

Sailing north past Gibraltar… Arlan kept watch until his Captain called him to the helm.

"To Marseilles?" said Arlan. "The fortified French port?"

"The place to kill a rat," said Lord Alecs, "is at the mouth of his hole!"

As he returned to his post, Arlan considered the life he had led and the peril that lay in the offing. Dr. Arlan de Borneo had run a successful medical practice in Dover until the unlucky day he botched a routine tonsillectomy on the town constable, rendering him aphonic for life. As a result his practice faltered, and he was  forced to seek employment at sea. The ships sailing under Captain Alecs of York had a long-standing reputation for being the most casualty-ridden in the fleet, and as a result the captain struggled to find physicians for his ship.

With no other options, Arlan accepted a post on the *Manhattan*, but because of his inordinate size and the limited crew that could subsequently be housed, he was obliged to perform the duties of a dozen men. Fortunately, it was a charge he was able to fulfill, for he could effortlessly clasp a line and pull with the force of twenty hands, and could labor for days without sleep. Although he was, by nature, a gentle soul, it was clear that if he were ever roused to anger, he would wreak more havoc than a regiment of Her Majesty's finest.

In the practice of his trade, Dr. Arlan was a proponent of natural remedies, having studied the salutary effects of the different foods, herbs and unguents he had discovered on his native Borneo. Foremost among his remedies was one born of his fondness for citrus, specifically his love of oranges. One afternoon when he was playing on the rocky coast of the island, he sliced his foot on a spike of coral. That evening he noticed his foot had become infected, and to relieve the burning he thrust it under a pile of peels discarded from a bushel of oranges. The dampness of the peels soothed the burning, and when he awoke the next morning his foot showed no sign of infection.

He practiced the cure on a number of neighbors, and soon verified the curative properties of moldy orange peels. He subsequently became interested in surgery, for which he developed an extraordinary dexterity with his trunk. He also possessed remarkable eyesight, and an astonishing memory which allowed him to repeat procedures he had seen only once, and to diagnose illnesses he had only read or heard about. These skills notwithstanding, he would have much preferred to live a peaceful and anonymous existence on shore, if his prodigious appetite had not required that he earn more than a handful of British crowns.

Aboard the *Manhattan* he was given the store room at the stern of the middle deck in which to sleep, but as he rarely slept, the space soon became a game room in which he and Captain Alecs passed slow hours in contests of two-king chess. The contests pleased and frustrated Lord Alecs, for he had never encountered a player whose skill rivaled his own, and though he won more than he lost, it seemed that luck played an inordinate role in his victories. Arlan enjoyed the matches as well, though for different reasons. It had only taken him a few games to unmask his Captain's strategy, a strategy based on aggression, in which

Alecs was willing to sacrifice any number of pieces if the maneuver brought an element of surprise and led to the rapid and dazzling defeat of his opponent. Once Arlan understood this, he was never surprised again, and from then on he was forced to lose matches on purpose to keep the tally leaning in the Captain's favor. The same aggressive maneuvers, Arlan understood, might be equally effective at sea, but only if Lord Alecs was unknown to the enemy. An astute commander who had engaged him before, and survived his first attacks, could redirect the aggression back to its source, and so, as the reputation of Lord Alecs and his tactics became better and better known, his career moved more swiftly to its end.

With all this in mind, Dr. Arlan de Borneo was not the least surprised when the *Manhattan* sailed directly past L'Isle d'If and straight toward the mouth of the Marseilles harbor, where it attacked the first ship it encountered, hoping to capture a crew member who would know the whereabouts of Blurtseau Lundif.

"Aaarrgghh!!!" growled Alecs. "Sixteen sheets to the wind!!! Into the devil's kiln!!"

"He's here!" said Echo, when they reached Marseilles.

But with the first mention of "Blurtseau Lundif" our bewildered heroes were whisked up the gangway of an enormous ship and deposited in a familiar place.

Echo did what she could to conceal her disappointment, and Winston did what he could to comfort her, but Winston's words were drowned by the stampede of footsteps above, and by the creaking timbers as the *Baleine* lumbered to sea.

No sooner had the ship set sail than it was engaged in battle, and when Echo and Winston thought their luck could not possibly get worse, a cannonball crashed through the hull, unleashing an avalanche of water into the hold.

Breathless, hopeless, and unconscious, our heroes were left for dead, until a powerful grey trunk darted in from above and snatched them from the frothing abyss.

"Who are these?" growled Lord Alecs.

"I found them floundering in the hold of the *Baleine*," said Harlan, "and brought them aboard."

"Very well," said Alecs, "they'll make a good meal for the men."

"A good meal!" screeched Winston. "I am Sir Winston Pig of Ashford Middlesex!"

"What?!" said Alecs. "Ashford? Subjects of the Queen? Very well, set them to swabbing the mizzen, and see if they last out the day."

Sensing that the two lost souls had a spirit kindred to his own, and feeling a filial responsibility after saving them from certain extinction, Dr. Arlan de Borneo decided to take Echo and Winston under his wing. He showed them the ropes, teaching them how to scrape and swab the deck, how to loose and haul the sails, how to man the pumps, and how to carry powder and cannon balls to the gun decks. Then, when it came time to man the rudder, he invited them to join him for evening conversation.

"What were you doing aboard the *Baleine*?" said Arlan.

"We had just arrived in Marseilles," said Winston, "when we were shanghaied after mentioning the name Blurtseau Lundif."

"Blurtseau Lundif?!" gulped Arlan.

"Yes," said Echo, "we've come to find him."

"But," said Arlan, "that's who Lord Alecs has come to kill!"

The elephant, donkey, and pig were gravely distressed to discover that Lord Alecs and Echo were each searching for the same Corsaire Extraordinaire, though for very different reasons. Echo related the story of her life with Blurtseau on her island, insisting upon his gentle and sympathetic nature, and though Arlan wanted to believe her, he protested that a reputation cannot be based on a total misrepresentation of facts, and that there must be some truth to the bloodthirsty tales. Echo admitted that Blurtseau had spoken of a number of conflicts, but that he always explained the reasons for his involvement, and his reasons seemed honest and sincere.

"In times of war," said Arlan, "what often seems black to one seems white to another, depending upon the vantage point from which it is viewed. Conflict, he continued, is a tricky business, filled with infinite, ever-changing shades of grey."

"Blurtseau," said Echo, "is the greyest animal I've ever known, there's not a single part of him that is entirely black or white."

"There's something to be said," said Arlan, "for animals that are grey."

Aboard ship, our heroes began to fit in. After years of acrobatics on her island, Echo quickly learned to swing and soar among the sails, while Winston, who suffered from a crippling fear of heights, found ways to be useful below.

The days passed, and the *Manhattan* kept vigil at the mouth of the port, lurking just behind the Isle d'If, attacking any vessel that ventured in or out, demanding that the Cowardly Corsaire present himself and engage Captain Alecs in direct and unbridled combat. But while business in Marseilles came to a halt, and the Napoleonic war machine ground its gears, the Corsaire Extraordinaire was nowhere to be found.

Slowly but surely, Echo and Winston began to convince Dr. de Borneo that Blurtseau Lundif was no worse than his own Captain Alecs, and that Blurtseau was probably the more sympathetic choice, if a choice was ever to be made.

Back in Roquebrune, Pableau and Zurrabela prepared
the terrace for the first crop of sugar beets.

"That was a good day's work," said Zurrabela.

"Yes it was," said Pableau.

"Why did it take you so long to put away the plow?" said Zurrabela.

"I went into the cottage," said Pableau, "and it looked like someone's been living there."

"Really?" said Zurrabela.

"Yes," said Pableau, "there were fresh cinders in the hearth and pumpkin rinds on the table."

"Pumpkins rinds?" said Zurrabela.

"Yes," said Pableau.

"Do you think it's wild animals?" said Zurrabela.

"No," said Pableau, "they're afraid of fire."

"Nevertheless," said Zurrabela, "take your axe the next time you go."

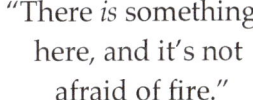
"There *is* something here, and it's not afraid of fire."

"What's that sound? It's a good thing I have an axe."

"Blurtseau?" said Pableau.
"Pableau?" said Blurtseau.

Two happier axe-wielding donkeys
the world has never seen.

"There was another donkey on the island?" said Pableau.

"Her name was Echo," said Blurtseau.

"You and Zurrabela seem happy," said Blurtseau.

"We are," said Pableau.

"Is it all you thought it'd be?" said Blurtseau.

"Yes," said Pableau, "for me it is."

"What's the best part?" said Blurtseau.

"Just being with her," said Pableau. "I do what I do, and she does what she does, and we're together at the bakery, and at the end of the day it seems like enough."

"Enough?" said Blurtseau.

"Yes," said Pableau, "the day is enough, the night is enough, the breeze and the sea and the trees, and the rain when it comes and the rain when it goes, the warmth and cold and animals, and even the humans rushing about... it all seems like enough."

"Did I mention," said Blurtseau, "her name was Echo?"

"The sea is at peace today," said Pableau.

"Yes," said Blurtseau.

"It's hard to believe it almost killed you," said Pableau.

"Yes," said Blurtseau.

"I suppose the floor of the sea is littered with dead sailors," said Pableau.

"Yes," said Blurtseau.

"But on the surface it appears so calm," said Pableau.

"Did I mention," said Blurtseau, "her name was Echo?"

"What do you want to do today?" said Pableau.

"I don't know," said Blurtseau. "What do you want to do?"

"The gulls are in fine form," said Pableau.

"Very fine," said Blurtseau.

"It's wonderful to see Blurtseau," said Zurrabela.

"Yes," said Pableau, "but I don't think he's going to stay."

"Why not?" said Zurrabela.

"I think he's in love," said Pableau.

"In love?" said Zurrabela.

"Yes," said Pableau, "with the donkey he met on the abandoned island. I think he's going to go live with her."

"On an abandoned island?"

"Yes," said Pableau.

"That's very romantic," said Zurrabela.

"Do you think I should put on a new roof?" said Pableau. "Mmmmm," said Blurtseau, "these sprouts are delicious."

"Très jolie," said Blurtseau.

"It's six o'clock now, and the sun is behind the bluff," said Blurtseau. "There are two more hours of indirect light before Nice glows pink and Monaco falls dark. The Grimaldis must be very sad to have lost control."

"Yes," said Pableau, "but the French must be very happy."

"Look at that ant," said Blurtseau, "he's carrying something twice his size."

"That's remarkable," said Pableau.

"Have you ever carried something twice your size?" said Blurtseau.

"Twice as big or twice as heavy?" said Pableau.

"Both," said Blurtseau.

"Yes," said Pableau.

"So have I," said Blurtseau.

"Why did you do it?" said Pableau.

"I didn't have any other choice," said Blurtseau.

"No," said Pableau, "neither did I."

"Are you going to return to Echo's island?" said Pableau.

"I've thought about it," said Blurtseau.

"Where is it?" said Pableau.

"It's off the coast of Italy," said Blurtseau, "I think they call it Montecristo."

"Montecristo?" said Pableau. "There's treasure on Montecristo."

"Really?" said Blurtseau.

"Yes," said Pableau, "pirate ships stash their booty in the caves."

"I didn't find any treasure," said Blurtseau.

"Maybe it's just a legend," said Pableau.

"Maybe," said Blurtseau.

"So you're going to return?"

"I don't know," said Blurtseau, "I'm not sure I'd be happy there."

"Why not?" said Pableau.

"Because when I was there," said Blurtseau, "I was always looking for a way to leave."

"Always?" said Pableau.

"Well, no," said Blurtseau, "not always. When I was with Echo I was happy to stay, but then she showed me a beached ship, and I immediately built a skiff and sailed away."

"How did she react?"

"She was very sad," said Blurtseau, "and so was I. As soon as I sailed beyond the surf, I longed to turn back."

"How would she feel if you went back now?"

"I don't know," said Blurtseau.

"Do you think that you were put on earth for a reason?" said Blurtseau.

"No," said Pableau, "I think my parents were just caught up in the moment."

"That's not what I mean," said Blurtseau. "I mean, do you think you have a destiny, a grand purpose to fulfill?"

"A grand purpose?" said Pableau. "You mean something the world can't do without?"

"Exactly," said Blurtseau. "Do you think you're here to do something that the world can't do without?"

"No," said Pableau.

As the days passed, Pableau and Blurtseau tended the garden at the cottage, Josette and Zurrabela took their paintings to Menton, and Claude smoked his pipe and conjured up visions of youth. Though the rising poverty in the region under the administration of the revolutionary "Alpes Maritimes" had forced the ladies to charge lower and lower prices for their canvasses, the group was confident that with the first crop of beets they would reopen the bakery and sell their pastries on a daily basis again.

One day, when Blurtseau was out walking…

"Blurtsoiselle?"

Blurtseau could not believe his eyes! Was it her? The fairest of fair, the sweetest of sweet, the…? He couldn't be sure, but before he had time to reflect, she began to speak. She had rehearsed the things she would say when she met Blurtseau again over and over in a hundred sleepless nights—how her life had begun a precipitous descent from the moment she wrote the infamous note declaring she was eloping with the cousin of the king, how she had been mistreated and subsequently abandoned, how she had struggled to survive in post-revolutionary Paris—but though she had rehearsed the tale a thousand times, in the emotion of the moment the words tumbled out in a frantic cacophony of disjointed and shapeless sounds, composed of run-on sentences, sudden starts and stops, and a torrent of incoherent thoughts.

Blurtseau listened to the excited ramblings of his former amour and managed to assemble the essence of the story she had told Pableau in Menton, but as he listened he couldn't help thinking of how he had abandoned Echo just as Blurtsoiselle had abandoned him, not for the cousin of a king, but for an equally empty promise, the pursuit of fortune and fame. He saw himself transformed into Blurtsoiselle, trying to explain not to himself but to Echo—on the day when they might meet—why he had abandoned a love that was simple and true.

Blurtsoiselle rattled on, stumbling and starting again and again, explaining her misguided reasons for what she had done, repeating how she had been deaf and dumb and blind, and how he had been right all along. And Blurtseau stood there, in the cool breeze and leafy shadows, with no chance to give voice to even the briefest expression of sympathy, until finally, with a desperate gulp of air, Blurtsoiselle finished her story, thanked Blurtseau for all he had given her, wished him well, and swiftly walked away.

As Blurtseau walked back to the villa, he considered the many failures of his life: his inability to keep his first love, his foolish abandonment of his second love, his frustrated career as a sea captain—exiled by the king and rejected by Napoleon—leaving him landlocked and shipless, with no prospect in the offing. Every major endeavor in his life had ended in ruins… but as he neared the villa, he looked up and spied Pableau on the terrace, watering his geraniums, and he remembered how empty the world had seemed when he had found the cottage empty, and had supposed his friends dead… and how overjoyed he had become when he found them wealthy and well… and suddenly he was filled with a sensation of completeness, and gratitude, and he felt his life was a complete success… an almost complete success. Only Echo was missing, and he could remedy that.

"I've got to find Echo!" said Blurtseau. No sooner were the words out of his mouth when a courrier knocked at the gate with a missive from Napoleon.

"What does it say?" said Pableau.

"It says," said Blurtseau, "that a bloodthirsty British sea captain, Lord Alecs of York, has sworn to meet me in battle, and until I present myself, he is sinking every French vessel that attempts to enter or leave the port of Marseilles. Bonaparte obliges me to report to the embattled harbor, captain a vessel, and put an end to Alecs of York."

"I'll make the necessary preparations to join you immediately," said Pableau.

"No," said Blurtseau, "the General writes my ship is already manned. Remain with Zurrabela, harvest your beets, and make the bakery prosper. I'll send word of my well-being as time permits. Give my regards to the others, and beg their forgiveness I was unable to take leave in person. Explain I have been called to serve, and must depart posthaste."

When Blurtseau arrived in Marseilles, the *Baleine*, repaired and reprovisioned, was waiting. Convinced he could vanquish the *Manhattan* force to force, the Corsaire sailed snout-first into the fray.

But the sides of the British ship, reinforced with bands of crucible steel, were impervious to the barrage of fire spitting from the decks of the *Baleine*.

Lord Alecs waited, withholding the signal to retaliate, until he saw a bolt of panic flash in his adversary's eyes. Then the signal came, and with it, a cloudburst of thirty-two pound raindrops…

"Merde…"

Aboard the *Manhattan* the crew was calm and composed, all except Winston, whose reaction to danger was to talk even more than usual, and talk more quickly, until he became a veritable Gatling gun of words, peppering the ears of everyone in range. It was no surprise then, when either by accident or on purpose, he was knocked to the gun deck, stuffed into a cannon, and discharged in the direction of the enemy ship...

"God save the Queen!"

Fortunately, the gunner's aim was high, and Winston sailed past the *Baleine's* main mast and into the sea beyond. Echo, watching from the foremast, saw him soar, still chattering as he went, and as soon as he hit the water she dove in and ferried him to a nearby plank.

When Winston regained his senses, he and Echo looked back to see the *Baleine* take a direct hit to the mainmast. The pole, splintered at the base, teetered, then crashed to the deck. Lord Alecs saw this as well and redoubled the volleys from his gun decks, sending rocket after rocket into the wounded *Baleine* until the ship keeled starboard, toppled to its side, and spun snout-first into the frothing sea.

The water was a cacophony of screaming voices and splashing limbs as the shipless crew scrambled for floating pieces of the *Baleine*. Echo strained to see if she could spy Blurtseau among them, but a wave from the undertow propelled her and Winston farther to sea, and all she could do was watch as the ever-smaller souls continued to scramble, and the *Manhattan*, now secure in its victory, retook its position behind the Isle d'If.

The next day Winston and Echo washed ashore on the uninhabited island of Ratonneau, just beyond the Isle d'If. Though they longed to return to Marseilles to hear what had become of Blurtseau, they were obliged to remain on the island for three weeks until they managed to hitch a ride to the continent.

Back in Marseilles, Blurtseau Lundif, who *had* survived the fray, was developing a new plan of attack. He now understood that the *Manhattan* could not be defeated in direct engagement; he decided he would have to secretly board the *Manhattan* and dispose of its captain in hoof to hoof combat. In order to do so, he would build a submergible.

Years before, when he was sailing in the service of the King, one of his men had spoken of a submergible vessel he had seen on a layover in Menorca. The British had called the vessel the "Turtle," and claimed it could sail underwater for as long as its pilot had oxygen to breathe. Blurtseau convinced the sailor to make a sketch of the vessel and Blurtseau had memorized the design for future use. The future was now.

Taking a dozen of his men, Blurtseau rigged out a cannonless fishing vessel which he sailed as close to the Isle d'If as Lord Alecs would allow. From there he lowered the "Tortue" into the moonlit water—the *Manhattan* having its guard down under a full moon—and sailed to the Isle d'If.

Cranking the propeller as fast as his stumpy legs could crank, he set a path to a small cove where he could dock unseen. But in his furious cranking, he consumed more oxygen than anticipated, and was forced to surface a hundred meters from shore. Happily, the maneuver went unnoticed, and he re-submerged and continued to the cove.

On shore his work was sudden, silent, and swift. He scaled the battlements, garroted the first guard, then the second, then the third, then he found the dinghy used to ferry men to the *Manhattan*, and set off rowing.

When Dr. Arlan de Borneo, keeping watch from the topmast, saw the dinghy making an unscheduled return to the *Manhattan*, he started to call to his captain, then, spying the long grey ears of Blurtseau Lundif and remembering the promise he had made to Echo and Winston, he stopped. His hesitation was decisive.

As soon as Blurtseau was aboard, the Corsaire moved like a scirocco through the ship, slaying everyone in sight. When he reached the captain's quarters, he kicked down the door, rousted the captain from bed, and quickly held him hostage with his own bare bodkin.

When the men saw the captain at the mercy of the invader, they immediately dropped their arms and consented to the Corsaire's demands. The sailors from Blurtseau's fishing vessel then came aboard, rope-tied the men above deck, and locked the rest below. At the first light of day, Blurtseau sailed the *Manhattan* into the rejoicing port of Marseilles…

The news of Blurtseau's victory spread like fire throughout the Republic. Marseilles had been liberated, Lord Alecs and his crew were in prison at the Chateau d'If, and the *Manhattan* was rigged out to sail for the French. It was a peerless success, and Blurtseau Lundif, Corsaire Extraordinaire and hero of France, was invited to Paris for a parade in his honor.

Mon cher Pableau,

By now you have certainly heard the news from Marseilles, and perhaps even of my parade in Paris. The nation has opened like an oyster before me, but I have nothing to give in return. Yes, the harbor is free, and Marseilles has returned to its business of commerce and war, but a hundred good men sleep in the hull of the sunken *Baleine*, and as many again wearing British blue. The conflict was prideful and pointless, yet I am praised for my courage. They say I have conquered death, but to conquer death you only have to die.

As I begin the journey home, I think of you. You who were there for my heartbreak in Paris, for my flight to Sagres, for my return to Roquebrune, and for countless hours at sea. It occurs to me that *you* are the true "Corsaire Extraordinaire," with your friendship, food, and song; ever faithful, ever true, ever Pableau. And so, as he departs this flag-draped capital, accept a warm embrace from the one whose life is a wasteland, is a living death, without you.

Yours faithfully,
a humble servant and friend,
Blurtseau L'un d'If

By the time Echo and Winston reached the continent, there was no one who did not know that Roquebrune was the home of Blurtseau Lundif.

"What are you going to say to him," said Winston, "when you see him?"

"If he's glad to see me," said Echo, "I won't have to say anything."

"And if he's not?" said Winston.
"Then," said Echo, "it won't matter what I say."

"Do you think it's unpatriotic," said Blurtseau, "to believe that fairness is the only thing worth fighting for?"

"Are you leaving for Echo's island?" said Pableau.
"Yes," said Blurtseau.
"What will you say when you see her?" said Pableau.
"A million things," said Blurtseau.
"Distance is a curious thing," said Blurtseau.
"How so?" said Pableau.
"Two beings," said Blurtseau, "can be alive and well at exactly the same time, but be galaxies apart, as if the other didn't exist, as if the other were not alive, or had never been alive. When I returned to Roquebrune and found the cottage empty, it was as if you were dead, even though you were just across the way. And

then there are all those other beings on the planet, the ones we've never met, the ones who have never existed in our lives, but still exist at exactly this same time."

"It makes our individual lives," said Pableau, "seem very very small."

"Yes," said Blurtseau, "and everything we know, seem like nothing."

"What do you think Echo is doing right now?" said Blurtseau.

"I don't know," said Pableau, "probably eating."

"Eating?" said Blurtseau.

"Yes," said Pableau, "donkeys are often eating."

"That's true," said Blurtseau. "Do you think she's thinking of me?"

"I don't know," said Pableau, "that probably depends on what she's eating."

"Whenever someone thinks of us," said Blurtseau, "it gives us a greater sense of existence—we exist in their mind and they exist on the planet, so we exist on the planet too."

"Yes," said Pableau.

"What do you think happens," said Blurtseau, "when no one ever thinks of us again?"

"I think," said Pableau, "that oblivion happens."

"Josette has done some paintings in your honor," said Pableau, "I think you'll like them."

"Le Capitaine L'un d'If se met son chapeau"

"I'm tired of human things," said Blurtseau.

"Human things?" said Pableau.

"Yes," said Blurtseau, "power, wealth, fame, and every other form of egotism pursued in the name of duty, honor, or personal development."

"Sounds like you're ready for Montecristo," said Pableau.

"Yes," said Blurtseau, "I'll get a boat ready tomorrow."

"Another day," thought Blurtseau, "and another night. The king is dead, and those who killed the king are dead, and Napoleon consolidates his power while those who would kill him wait in the wings. And the once-full moon that illuminated my vainglorious victory now wanes with a warbling light. Tomorrow the fighting will begin anew, the British, French, Spanish, Dutch, German, Italian, Sardinian, Greek generals... and all the world spins with the bones of the living and the bones of the dead, so many dead, those who pursued a borrowed or inherited dream, white bones in the soil, white bones in the surf of the sea, bones as white as the flickering tail of the waning moon, sparking and submerging among the breakers, flickering water reflection of fleeting sun echoed upon half-eaten moon, half-eaten moon half-eclipsed by the globe it now reflects down upon... half-eaten glow that grows dimmer each day... until the moon, the day, the night, and all our blood-urgent exploits fall dark upon the darkness of the sea, and vanish in the low laving sound of the waves eating the rocks with their dance of disintegration.

"And when the moon goes black, the stars will mark my path to Montecristo where Echo, alone on her island, watches the same silver flicker on a different surface of the same sea. And the light that flickered in *her* heart? Has it fallen prey to the same dance of deterioration? Will I find the moon already extinguished in the sea of her breast? Eclipsed by the vainglorious sphere that was my haste to depart? The misguided course of this star-crossed corsair pursuing a sinking star? Yesterday's hero is the dark side of the earth facing the dark side of the moon, is darkness double, two-faced night's faceless faces, an echo of existence which touches no ear, a shout across an infinite expanse, an unreciprocated smile, a source without destination, a word from the heart that never arrives."

"My heart is an echo of the disintegration
of the heart of the universe
that penetrates and disintegrates my own heart."

"I think we made it," said Winston.

The next day, when Blurtseau was out walking…

"Echo?"

As soon as he saw her Blurtseau began to tell her how right she had been and how wrong he had been and… no sooner did he begin when he realized he was saying exactly what Blurtsoiselle had said in the same jumbled fashion, so he stopped, took a long look in her eyes, and said, "I missed you." Echo, in turn, looked into his eyes and repeated, "I missed you."

Then the two sat, without saying another word, while the light slipped through the leaves, the birds called across the coast, and the breeze licked and tickled their ears.

Echo and Winston's arrival brought with it the story of Dr. Arlan de Borneo, and his role in Blurtseau's full-moon espionage. A short note to the jailor at the Château d'If was sufficient to procure his release and reward him with a first-class passage to Roquebrune.

Once the newcomers were safely situated, Echo and Blurtseau took their leave and, promising to establish a regular mail route between Montecristo and the Italian mainland, set sail for Echo's island.

Pableau and Zurrabela, desirous to stay near their crop of beets, returned to the cottage….

Doctor de Borneo set up shop in Roquebrune…

Josette got back to work…

Winston tutored his disciples…

And Lord Alecs of York plotted his revenge
in a windowless cell of the Château d'If.

The End

I like it, said Alex, especially the battles, and the dashing young sea captain, Alecs of York.

www.ingramcontent.com/pod-product-compliance
Lightning Source LLC
Chambersburg PA
CBHW040559240426
43664CB00047B/1